Sewing Tools & Trinkets

Collector's Identification & Value Guide

Volume 2

Helen Lester Thompson

COLLECTOR BOOKS

A Division of Schroeder Publishing Co., Inc.

Cover design by Beth Summers

Book design by Mary Ann Hudson

COLLECTOR BOOKS
P.O. Box 3009
Paducah, Kentucky 42002-3009

www.collectorbooks.com

Copyright © 2002 Helen Lester Thompson

The current values in this book should be used only as a guide. They are not intended to set prices, which vary from one section of the country to another. Auction prices as well as dealer prices vary greatly and are affected by condition as well as demand. Neither the author nor the publisher assumes responsibility for any losses that might be incurred as a result of consulting this guide.

Searching For A Publisher?

We are always looking for people knowledgeable within their fields. If you feel that there is a real need for a book on your collectible subject and have a large comprehensive collection, contact Collector Books.

Contents

Dedication 4

Acknowledgments 4

Credits 4

About the Author 5

Introduction 6

Sewing Stands, Kits & Baskets 7

Darners & Clamps 27

Needles & Pins, Holders & Cushions 41

Thimbles & Holders 69

Thread: Holders, Winders, Spools & Stands 85

Assorted Tools & Toys 93

Scissors, Knives & Cutters, Tape Measures, Rulers & Gauges .109

Mauchline, Tartan & Tunbridge Ware 123

Chatelaines & Accessories 129

Sewing Tools: Representative Items of Collections 137

Glossary 159

Bibliography 160

Dedication

To my husband, John, and our eclectic, blended family

&

In memory, with love, of my good friend Lee Draughon Brown.

Acknowledgments

My sincere appreciation to each of the sewing tool collectors and dealers who contributed their time and the loan of some of their outstanding collection pieces. Your sharing added to the quality of the book and my pleasure in putting it together.

Faye Beckwaite
Wendie Blackey
Peggy Carroll
Bonnie Erney
Faye Foster
Ann and John Gallo
Mollie Heron
Betty Hoopes
Betty Hudson
The Kentucky Museum, Western Kentucky University
Louise Knight
Tom Mullaney
Jeannette Kunz
Dan McGehee

Paula Moore
Mary Nehring
Pam Osborne
Joan Pappas
Sally Potashnick
Julie Powell
Gerald Roy
Charles Souder
Shirley Stewart
Kathlyn Sullivan
Donogene Thurmond
Peter Weiss

Credits

Photographs of book cover and chapter facings: Richard Walker

Photographs of Faye Beckwaith and Ruth Broughton collections: Richard Walker

Photographs of chapter sewing tool layouts: Charles R. Lynch

Contents

Dedication 4

Acknowledgments 4

Credits 4

About the Author 5

Introduction 6

Sewing Stands, Kits & Baskets 7

Darners & Clamps 27

Needles & Pins, Holders & Cushions 41

Thimbles & Holders 69

Thread: Holders, Winders, Spools & Stands 85

Assorted Tools & Toys 93

Scissors, Knives & Cutters, Tape Measures, Rulers & Gauges 109

Mauchline, Tartan & Tunbridge Ware 123

Chatelaines & Accessories 129

Sewing Tools: Representative Items of Collections 137

Glossary 159

Bibliography 160

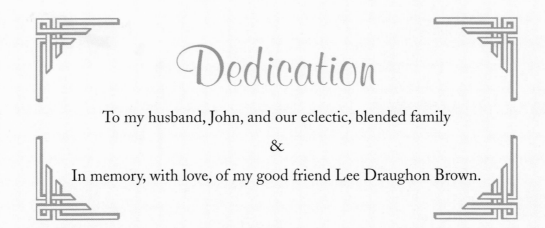

Dedication

To my husband, John, and our eclectic, blended family

&

In memory, with love, of my good friend Lee Draughon Brown.

Acknowledgments

My sincere appreciation to each of the sewing tool collectors and dealers who contributed their time and the loan of some of their outstanding collection pieces. Your sharing added to the quality of the book and my pleasure in putting it together.

Faye Beckwaite
Wendie Blackey
Peggy Carroll
Bonnie Erney
Faye Foster
Ann and John Gallo
Mollie Heron
Betty Hoopes
Betty Hudson
The Kentucky Museum, Western Kentucky University
Louise Knight
Tom Mullaney
Jeannette Kunz
Dan McGehee

Paula Moore
Mary Nehring
Pam Osborne
Joan Pappas
Sally Potashnick
Julie Powell
Gerald Roy
Charles Souder
Shirley Stewart
Kathlyn Sullivan
Donogene Thurmond
Peter Weiss

Credits

Photographs of book cover and chapter facings: Richard Walker

Photographs of Faye Beckwaith and Ruth Broughton collections: Richard Walker

Photographs of chapter sewing tool layouts: Charles R. Lynch

Sewing Stands, Kits & Baskets

The evolution of sewing containers from simple cloth or leather bags resulted in a wide variety of sizes and shapes, as well as materials used. By the 1700s sewing tools were made for the gentry and royalty by highly skilled jewelers and metal craftsmen. The materials were precious metals, gems, and designs were intricately executed. One of the most popular materials was mother-of-pearl, its fragile beauty had a lot of appeal.

As an economic middle class became part of society, a market grew for practical, attractive, and affordable sewing containers that fit the lifestyle. For the most part the items manufactured for this economic group were well made and durable.

The étui from France, and the lady's companion from England and Germany were very popular. They were small, outfitted with the necessary tools for travel or a day with a sewing group. They contained scissors, needle case, bodkin, and thimble as the basics. There were variations depending on the size, including a mirror, small perfume, lady's knife, a small New Testament, tweezers, and a small button hook. The boxes and kits were made of wood, leather, ivory, and often lined with silk or velvet. The larger boxes were two or three sectioned layers.

The history of baskets and their many uses coincides with man's development. Families, tribes, as well as individuals, used natural materials such as grass, rushes, willow, honeysuckle, bamboo, and small tree canes. These are just a few examples. Some were lined, some the pincushion, scissors sheath, and thimble holders were attached to the inside of the basket. These were particularly popular in the first quarter of the twentieth century. Sewing kits, boxes, and baskets are of interest to many collectors as seen in the "Collectors" chapter.

France; Two Eiffel Tower sewing kits; pincushions fill arches; French tools and needles; c. 1890; base 3½" x 6½", tower 5½" x 2½"; Blue and red velvet; $350.00 – 400.00 each.

Top row:

1–4. England; Lady's companion; leather; assorted tools; made for day's outing or a holiday trip; in addition to tools a mirror, a small copy of the New Testament, and a single blade knife might be included.

    1, 2. Four tools; steel trim, decorative settings, c. 1840; $100.00 – 190.00 each.

    3. Thread storage in bottom layer, tools in top; c. 1850; $250.00.

    4. Gold trim; c. 1875; "A prize given by E. Wilder"; $210.00.

5. France; étui, gilded sterling; sides covered with shagreen dyed green (shark skin), decorated with silver medallion on both sides; eight tools all but one piece French; c. 1860; 1½"w x ½"d x 3½"h; $1,800.00.

Row two:

1, 3, 4. England; Leather covered lady's companion in gold lettering; c. 1840 – 1875; $150.00 – 170.00 each.

2. England; painted wood étui, top is thread holder with eyelet for thread release, middle thimble holder, base telescopes off and holds pins and needles; c. 1875; $125.00.

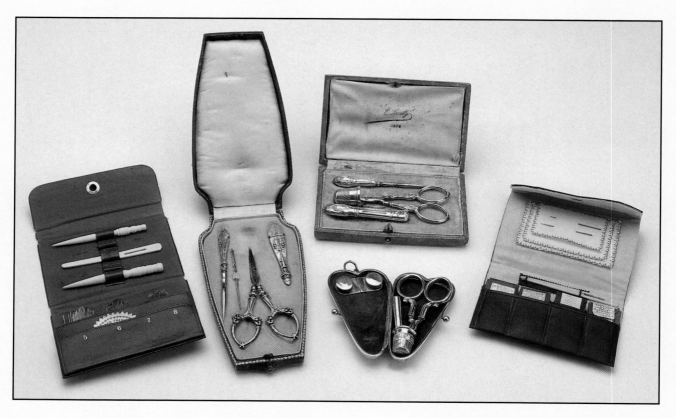

Top row:
1. England; red leather hinged kit with two ivory punches, bodkin, and needle pocket; c. 1900; 3" x 4"; $50.00.
2. France; sewing kit, five pieces, thimble missing; gilded over sterling; leather box with silk lining; c. 1850; $235.00.
3. France; leather box sewing kit, silk lining says "E. Bailey," tools HM sterling, thimble monogram "Addie," needle case, punch, scissors; c. 1880; $235.00.
4. England; sterling heart shaped sewing kit, velvet lining; pair of thread winders, needle case, thimble, scissors; c. 1911; 1½" x 2¼"; $295.00.
5. USA, Shaker, New England; fold-up, red leather with gold silk lining; two buttonhole stitched wool needle pages; bone bodkin, ivory punch in pocket, four packages of needles, brass snap closer; 3" x 4"; $90.00.

The Best of Sears Collectibles
1905 – 1910, 1976

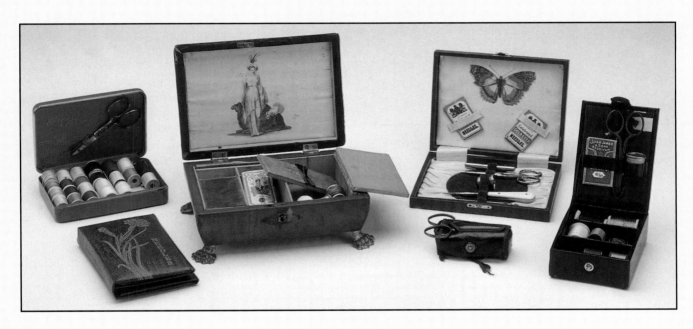

Top row:
1. USA; thread box with scissors; labeled "Coats and Clark ONT"; German scissors, leatherette covering; small spools of cotton and silk thread; c. 1930; $15.00.
2. England; red leather sewing box with pressed brass lion's feet; lady standing in front of seated camel pictured on silk lining; four divided sections containing needle box, pincushion, spools of thread, and key that locks the box; brass oval on box top reads "Julia M. Anderson"; c. 1900; 3" x 5" x 7"; $90.00.
3. England; maroon leather sewing box, silk lining with colorful butterfly stencil; needle case, scissors, needle bodkin, crochet hook, thimble, bone and sterling; c. 1901; $75.00.
4. USA; navy leather covered sewing box, velvet lining; top fitted with needles, scissors, brass thimble; divided area with silk thread, pins, and needles; 1915; $30.00.

Row two:
1. Czechoslovakia; leatherette fold-up kit, hand-painted flowers and needles on cover; "Art work Needles" Patent date 1914; 3" x 5"; $20.00.
2. USA, Canterbury, New Hampshire, Shaker; small "bronzed leather" sewing kit; J. Rogers scissors in sheath on top; lined with rust silk; two buttonhole stitched wool pages for needles, three spools of thread, brass thimble; 1½" x 3"; $125.00.

1. USA; walnut, slant top divided with pull knobs and carrying handle, footed; c. 1920; $30.00.
2. USA, New England; information inside box, "made by novitiates of the East Poland Settlement of the Maine Sabbathday Lake Shakers." This settlement was abandoned in early 1900s. These boxes were made for "the World People." They originally had cardboard inserts, but many have been lost. The box is lined with a printed cotton fabric; the outside of the top has a beautiful wood inlay top; 3" x 8" x 11"; $75.00.
3. England; young girl's sewing box, brown leather, silk lining, nine sewing tools displayed on inside of top; some personal items in box, comb, 1872 coin, compact, photos, fabric coin holder, cast-iron scissors; c. 1880; 2" x 3½" x 4½"; $120.00.
4. USA; sewing box, red velvet; bone tools displayed on inside of lid; in the box a card reads "Remember Me"; buttons, thread, package of needles and pins; c. 1910; 3" x 5" x 6"; $58.00.

Top row:
1. USA, New York; two tiers with pincushion on top; the pincushion acts as pull to lift the lid; eight spools of thread housed in top; bone eyelets for easy thread access; drawer for tool storage, maple knob; 5½" x 7" x 5½"; $150.00.

Row two:
1. England; wooden box decorated with sea shells, heart-shaped pincushion edged with small shells; decorative paper on sides; souvenir items throughout coastal Europe and England; c. 1875; $65.00.
2. France; wood and glass oval sewing box, pincushion on top; spools of thread and winders inside; souvenir; c. 1890; 2½" x 5"; $125.00.

Clockwise:
1. USA, Maine, Native American; three-dimensional design; octagonal "cane" woven side pockets; there may have been a top originally; c. 1900; $75.00.
2. USA; braided sweet grass; removable "plate" with pin and needle books, thimble holder, scissors, thread holder, attached; c. 1915; $88.00.
3. USA; lined with pink satin, drawstring bag; attached inside top, thimble holder and thimble, pincushion, scissors and sheath; c. 1920; $80.00.
4. USA; double braid, sweet grass sewing basket; filled with sewing tools, thread, yarn, small pieces of fabrics; c. 1915; $70.00.

Top row:
1, 2, 4. USA; roll-ups made of cloth; handmade.
   1. Pennsylvania; two storage pockets; c. 1860; $60.00.
   2. Hand-quilted soft print fabric; one pocket, wool pages for needles; c. 1875; $48.00.
3. Bronzed leather; cotton print lining, double pincushion, one pocket; wool pages for pins and needles; c. 1910; $98.00.
   4. Cover made of silk with pull-thread work; lined with white wool fabric; finished-edge embroidery; c. 1915; $75.00.

Row two:
1. USA; tooled leather, silk tie; one pocket, wool pages for needles; monogram "A.R."; silk lining; c. 1920; $28.00.

Row three:
1. USA; beaded roll-up; Native American work, Northern Plains; glass beads; c. 1920; $25.00.
2. USA; cloth book for storing sewing tools; handmade, embroidered, and bound; eight "pages"; cover of book embroidered "A Friend in Need"; c. 1915; $65.00.
3. USA; black silk, wool lined roll-up; one pocket with leather pincushion; c. 1920; $70.00.

Clockwise:
1. USA; oak split basket; with tape measure, plastic thimble, bone punch, small heart-shaped pincushion; c. 1940; 3" x 2"; $5.00.
2. USA; beautiful printed silk sewing bag, green silk handles; sweet grass thimble holder, thread box, scissor sheath; pincushion basket; sterling scissors, brass thimble, sterling handle oval darner, thread and needles; c. 1915; $75.00.
3. USA; sewing carry-all, printed rayon, machine stitched binding; houses bobbins, spools of thread, plastic thimble, brass safety pins; c. 1940; $8.00.
4. USA; handmade felt sewing kit, appliqué flowers and leaves; Talon zipper, pinked edges, wool pages for pins and needles; bone punch and bodkin; c. 1945; $7.00.

1. Tabletop storage for sewing items; drawers read from top, "Pins," "Needles," "Buttons," and have brass pulls; cat sitting on top; c. 1875; $200.00.
2. USA; sewing kit; button hook and scissors joined with screw to thread winder, difficult to use because of size; folds onto winder; "Pat, April 4, 1914" TM "Hesuah"; $8.00.

These small sewing kits were designed for travel, taking up very little space. They are figural and whimsical. Materials used include wood-stained and natural celluloid of a number of different colors. They are products of USA, Germany, France, and Italy, c. 1900 – 1935.

Top row:
1. USA; steel "flask," pins and needles on either side of brass thimble; $8.00.
2. Italy; "lady" kit; hat is a thimble, red shaft holds thread winder with needles inside; painted face; 2½"; $75.00.
3. USA; natural and painted wood, sewing egg; holds thread, pins, needles, small scissors, thread winder; c. 1900; $48.00.
4. Germany; silhouette of man and woman transfer; opening in top for an aluminum thimble; push the thimble and it forces the bottom to release sewing kit; stamped "DRGM Weber E1," in pencil a former owner's name, "Alice Boutemann"; c 1900; $35.00.
5. France; green Bakelite with tassel and painted white swan; original marbleized display box; stamped "made in France"; thimble screw top, thread winder, and cylinder for needles; original display box; c. 1930; 3"; $68.00.
6. France; yellow Bakelite; transfer Japanese scene; original display box; screw top thimble, thread winder, and needle cylinder; printing on box "LA Couseuse épouse CB Paris"; souvenir; c. 1905; 3"; $75.00.

Row two:
1. USA; sewing kit; yellow Bakelite; screw top thimble, empty winder, and needle case; c. 1920; 3"; $5.00.
2. France; sewing kit, Bakelite, with penguin painted; stamped "made in France"; c. 1915; 2¼"; $50.00.
3. England; sewing kit egg, gilt over brass; needles, pins, and thread; c. 1900; $45.00.

The term "sewing caddy" is an old name given to a variety of figural sewing kits. This group is different animal shapes, chickens being the most popular, but other animals were represented as seen in the photograph. The handmade caddy has unique design choices. Placement of sewing tools, scissor blades representing the beak, were for convenience and display. They are very popular with collectors. These pieces are a few from an interesting collection belonging to an Illinois school teacher who lives on a farm.

Top row:
1. USA; white rabbit seated on stand, painted wood, handmade; pincushion tail, thread on spindles, scissors housed in ears, thimble between front paws; c. 1930; $58.00.
2. USA; large chicken (sex undetermined) on stand, wood, handmade, and hand painted; thread and thimble on hexagon stand, scissors lower neck, missing pincushion on back; c. 1930; $65.00.

Row two:
1. USA; small bird caddy on octagonal stand with a storage drawer steel pull, wood; thread and thimble on stand, scissors through head; commercially made; c. 1935; $48.00.
2. USA; ghost town in southwest souvenir; wood donkey on painted stand; six spindles, two spools of thread, colorful pincushion in "basket"; c. 1920; $38.00.

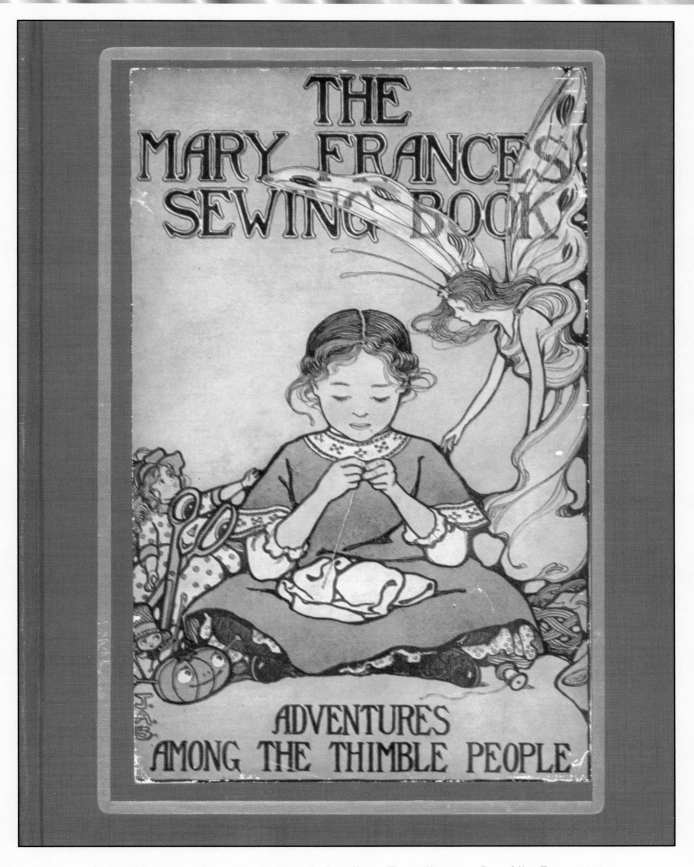

Cover of *The Mary Frances Sewing Book,* by Jane Eayre Fryer; illustrator, Jane Allen Bayer, 1913.

Beautifully crafted from salvage pieces; drawer facing is from treadle sewing machine, chair trim, wood top trimmed to fit, walnut; seated duck, head holding scissors, pincushion on back, four spindles with thread; c. 1900; $95.00.

Delightful New England sewing "Puppet," handmade; bone earrings with small brass safety pins; embroidered face and collar edge, decorative glass beads; ribbon arms and legs, bone rings with safety pins, darning thread on one arm, spools on legs; silk ribbon hanger; c. 1940; $90.00.

Snowshoe sewing kit; hand-made, wood frame, string webbing, velvet space with chenille wrap and anchoring for tools; bone needle holder, bodkin, two crochet hooks, punch, steel needle bodkin ball tip; chenille hanger; c. 1910; $125.00.

France; sewing or "dust" doll; wood head and hands, stained and painted face; hat, lace collar, dress made from French materials; soft arms, paddle-shaped hands; black grosgrain ribbon threads through head and attaches to pink storage bag, seen at edge of the skirt, doll is hung by the ribbon when not in use and bag is drawn up under the skirt out of sight; c. 1900; $200.00.

Japan, Osaka, TM Sichitokukakehari; Keyaki wood; this style box was more affordable for average families in Japan; the thread holder lifts out and is stored in the box, the cover to lower right stores snippet and soft items; longer lower drawer for fabric scraps from kimonos; others have tools, reading glasses; it is solid wood; c. 1912 – 1927; $300.00.

Modern Priscilla: A Magazine for Women, June 10, 1910.

Japan; beautiful grained Kaiki wood; constructed with bamboo nails — very thin, barely visible; variety of iron pulls from knobs to swing handles; pincushion covered with coarse cotton fabric and stuffed with human hair; pincushions were often covered with three layers of cloth; drawers storing kimono scraps, thread, tool to hold kimono fabric tight while stitching; this style and size sewing box was generally found in more affluent households; c. 1850, Taisho era box, heavy grain; 9" x 8" x 10¼"; $550.00.

England; lady's companion; green leather, gold lettering, tropical birds, fountains, and flowering vines; red leather needle holder, sterling handle punch and scissors, ornate design on knife and one blade; thimble HM Birmingham, sterling, 1913, size 18. Rd1719159, RC & SL; four storage units, waffle and flower design; plaid paper covered drawer, silver pull, and ivory thread waxer; 1¾" x 3" x 4"; $400.00.

Comfort Kits for   Army and Navy

Three styles selected by the Red Cross as especially adapted to men in active service and in hospitals. Should be made of plain khaki-color twill. It is recommended that the kits be marked with an American flag sewn or embroidered on the outside.

Completed articles should be sent to the nearest Red Cross chapter if possible. When this cannot be done they should be sent to the Red Cross Division Supply Service in the nearest of the following cities: Boston, New York, Philadelphia, Washington, Atlanta, New Orleans, St. Louis, Chicago, Cleveland, Denver, Minneapolis, and San Francisco.

COMFORT KIT NO. 1. SEE DIAGRAMS DIRECTLY BELOW

Articles in Comfort Kit No. 1

*A 1 and A 3. — Thread, heavy white and waxed khaki-color (sometimes called carpet or button thread), wound on cards.

On the outside of these pockets sew six khaki-color buttons, size for uniforms, six khaki buttons, shirt size, also six white buttons for underwear.

A 2. — Needles assorted large sized in case; thimble large size celluloid; sewing wax.

B. — Tobacco pouch and tobacco.

C 1. — Tooth powder in tin container.

C 2. — Folding knife and spoon.

C 3. — Soap in metal or celluloid box.

C 4. — Handkerchiefs, two or three, must be khaki-color. On outside of pocket pin 12 No. 3 black safety pins and 6 khaki-color patent trouser buttons.

D 1. — Shaving brush or safety razor.

D 2. — Shaving soap and blades.

D 3. — Comb, preferably metal, in case.

D 4. — Pipe.

E 1. — Playing-cards or other game.

E 2. — Mouth organ.

E 3. — Wash-cloth.

F. — Writing materials, pencil, and pair of heavy socks, hand or machine knitted.

DIAGRAM No. 1 FOR COMFORT KIT No. 1
Use Section A for pockets on Flap No. 1; Section B for pocket B; Section C for pockets C 1-2-3; Section D for pocket C on Flap No. 2 and pockets D 1-2-3-4.

These Comfort Kits may be had stamped on khaki-color material. See page 33.

DIAGRAM No. 2 FOR COMFORT KIT No. 1

* Such supplies as are khaki-color for the Army are black for the Navy.

Comfort Kit No. 1 (For Service Use)

ONE-HALF yard 36-inch material, 4 yards of tape for binding; one small American flag to be sewed on the outside of kit. These flags can be purchased cheaply in the form of ribbon, about 24 flags to the yard.

Cut out sections A, B, C, and D as indicated on Diagram No. 1. From these pieces make the applied pockets of the case, some flat, others slightly full, as shown on Diagram No. 2.

Fold in selvage ends of goods to form series of pockets marked E E E and large pocket marked F. Bind all edges neatly with stout tape. Attach ties of tape to flaps 1 and 2 so they can be brought together and tied over the pockets. Attach ties of tape on outside of case at H and J. These ties should be long enough to go twice around kit and keep all secure; two loops of tape should be added as shown in diagram No. 2, that the whole kit may be hung up evenly balanced.

It is important that the openings of the pockets B, C, and D face the loops, so that small articles will not fall out when the case is hung. Snappers sewn at the edge of the pockets E and F will help to make their contents more secure.

Comfort Kit No. 2 (For Service Use)

One-third yard 27-inch material, 30 inches of tape for draw-string, and an American flag for marking the outside.

Fold and sew up into a simple bag, 12 inches square with an inch hem at the top through which is run the gathering-string of tape.

Sewing materials are attached to a hemmed piece of canton flannel, 3 x 12. The upper edge is sewed into hem at inside top of bag. A single snap sewed at top and bottom of the strip, as shown at A and B in diagram, brings the two ends of the strip together, protecting the contents. This kit should contain the same articles as No. 1.

Comfort Kit No. 3 (For Hospital Use)

Especially designed to be pinned to the side of a bed and contains the small things which a wounded man will want to keep near him.

Two yards of 27-inch material will make two kits. Two and one-half yards of tape are needed for binding and tie-ends for each case. Stork sheeting, 9 x 13½ inches, is required to line pockets D for toilet articles.

Measure and tear the entire strip of goods lengthwise. Then tear sidewise from the strip the following pieces for the pockets: *Pocket A* — 7¼ inches torn; 6½ inches finished, allowing ⅜ inch for turning in at bottom, and narrow hem at top. *Pockets B 1-5* — 4 inches torn; 3¼ inches finished. *Pockets C 1-3*— two strips 5 inches torn, 4¼ inches finished; the extra fulness is needed to make the plaits. Piecing the goods for this series of pockets may be avoided by tearing off two 5-inch strips the full width of the material before dividing it lengthwise for the rest of the kit.

Souvenir Pocket.

DIAGRAM No. 4 FOR COMFORT KIT No. 3

Comfort Kit No. 3 (continued)

To make the pockets D 1-D 5, face the lower end of the long strip of goods with the 9-inch piece of stork sheeting, sewing both sides of the sheeting firmly to the kit before hemming and turning up the flap, which is then divided into pockets as indicated on diagram No. 4.

Hem upper edge of strips for C 1-3, plait and attach to case 1 inch above pockets D 1-5.

Hem strips for pockets A and B and apply B to A, sewing the partition seams in B before attaching both pockets at once to case, 1 inch above pockets marked C.

Almost every soldier has a little collection of souvenirs. The Souvenir Pocket is intended to hold these and other personal effects. Hem upper end of strip of which kit is being made, and fold over a flap 12 inches when finished. While in use this large flap pocket is turned back and hangs behind the bag, but if the soldier wishes to take his kit with him on leaving the hospital its contents can be made secure by bringing the flap forward over the small pockets and fastening it down by snaps sewn to X, Y, and Z. The whole kit can then be rolled up and tied as the contents permit.

Bind the side edges of the kit securely with the tape and attach tie ends on the outside of the point marked H. The kit is fastened to the mattress of the bed by 2 large safety-pins at the upper corners.

Contents of Comfort Kit No. 3

Souvenir pocket for personal effects.

A. Writing materials, pencil, etc.

B. Pipe, cigarette paper, tobacco pouch, and tobacco.

C. Handkerchiefs, playing-cards, and metal mirror.

D. Tooth-paste, tooth-brush, shaving-brush and soap, wash-cloth.

Safety-pins and sewing materials may be attached to the outside of any of these pockets, though these supplies will probably not be much needed in hospitals.

Do not include chewing-gum, chocolate, mouth organ, or sharp instruments, such as scissors or knives.

DIAGRAM No. 3 FOR COMFORT KIT No. 2

USA; American "gothic" style sewing box; walnut, maple trim; top: pincushion, push catch to open; center: just above first key hole, drop mirror, mounted on board twelve metal thread reels; set in just below mirror a sectioned sewing box that can be lifted out, top: inlay geometric pattern; small keyhole pull drawer; when everything is closed it is not obvious that the box has three sections; 13½"h x 16" w x 11½"d; good condition; c. 1860; $1,200.00.

USA, Delaware, Ohio; sewing stand, maple, handcrafted; top: covered, twelve spindle spool holder; 10" across; center: flayed open basket for fabric and yarn, skeins of wool yarn; 15" across; bottom: platform, four turned legs, 15" across turned center post; very good condition; $390.00.

Left:
USA, New England; split cane basket, some color; 13" across, 5" deep, four side woven pockets; c. 1920; $48.00.

Right:
USA, New England; woven sweet grass and split canes, top with a ring; 3" across, 2¼" deep; good condition; c. 1940; $38.00.

Darners & Clamps

Darners

Darners were a necessity in order to keep clothing in usable condition. Historically darners of many sizes and shapes as well as materials evolved as a result of what was available. Gourds, smooth rocks, and wood were early objects. Handcrafted and commercial darners were adapted to suit the needs of small to large items. The egg shape is the best known but soon there were foot forms, round balls with short handles, mushrooms, flat discs, German darning wooden dolls, and eggs with and without handles. Wood was the most common material they were made of, but glass, metal, celluloid, ceramic, and plastic were used, with some painted, some stained, and some natural. The more expensive darners had plain and decorative sterling handles, Russian enamel, and semi-precious stones. Amethyst was a popular stone.

Darning was a simple weaving technique. It was important to execute the weaving of a worn area so that it was smooth and strong, necessary for comfort and the life of the garment. After WWII the cost and availability of socks, gloves, and work clothes made darners in most homes no longer necessary — a sigh of relief from many young girls.

The wood darners were made not only in the USA but also in England, Germany, and Scotland. During the 1920s – 1930s, they were often packaged in attractive boxes with a ditty to bring a smile. Glass darners were blown and molded, many different colors can be found. Some of the prettiest ones are peach blow and varieties of end of day. They are worth the high cost. Some darners have removable handles for storing needles and pins. The glove darners have a small egg shape at one end and an almost round shape at the other end. Larger egg shaped darners often house a complete sewing kit, thread, needles, pins, thimble, and scissors.

Many enjoy collecting darners, their shapes, material, and origin make them interesting.

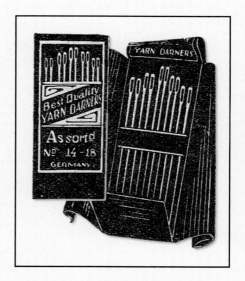

Baltimore Price Reducer, Nov. 1927.

Baltimore Price Reducer, October 1926.

Top row:
1. England; two colors of wood, walnut, sycamore; tunbridge; c 1880; 9½";
   $100.00.

Row two:
1. USA; wood; removable handle for thimble and needles, c. 1885; 6" (see single
   item photo page 31); $54.00.
2. USA; oval painted wood; sterling handle Unger Bros., "925 fine," plain;
   monogram "N.L.F."; c. 1920; 5½"; $95.00.
3. USA; wood mushroom; hollow handle for pins and needles; c. 1910; 4½";
   $25.00.

Row three:
1. USA; turned wood, one piece, dome top, tapered handle; c. 1900; 6½";
   $50.00.
2. USA, West Virginia; glass, hand blown, soft pink; c. 1920; 5½"; $54.00.
3. USA; hand-blown glass, six colors known as "end of day"; 6" (see single item
   photo page 31); $100.00.
4. USA; clear glass, small darner with turned handle; used for lightweight and
   knitted items; c. 1910; 4½"; $38.00.
5. USA; amethyst glass, pestle shape; used for small items; 4"; $70.00.

Top row:
1. USA; "Double Darn"; wood, round foot and small mushroom shape; c. 1985; 7"; $38.00.
2. Germany; wood; hollow screw handle; advertising on top, "Art. 50," "Darner and Needle Case," "C registered."; c. 1910; 4½"; $39.00.
3. USA; black painted wood, glove darner, corn flower painted on handle; attached to original display card "Gloves of kid & gloves of wool, Gloves of silk & cotton, too, Often need a little mending; So this mender I am Sending"; c. 1920; $58.00.

Row two:
1. Germany; wood, painted, pansy on top; used for small items; removable handle for pins and needles; c. 1920; 4½"; $70.00.
2. USA; walnut egg darner, telescope top stores tools; c. 1870; 3" x 2¼"; $35.00.

Row three:
1. England; turned walnut, one piece; elongated mushroom; c. 1900; 4½"; $12.00.
2. USA; wood, flat top, short handle; c. 1915; 4"; $10.00.
3. England; turned wood, one piece; walnut end, oval top, c. 1900; 9"; $38.00.
4. USA; painted wood; 1½" sterling medallion attached to lower edge of handle; c. 1920; 5½"; $35.00.
5, 8. England; wood; double ended glove darner; c. 1900; 3½";
   5. $20.00.
   8. Painted black; $20.00.
6, 7, 9, 10. USA; glove darners, one egg larger than the other; note the difference; 4½".
   6, 7, 9. Enameled wood; $15.00 – 25.00.
   10. Sterling holder, enameled wood ends; $90.00.
11. England; sterling, Birmingham; 1910; $100.00.

1. USA; "maiden form"; natural wood; unusual; needle scratches visible on both ends; c. 1900; 5½"; $60.00.
2. Scotland; Mauchline ware; two colors of painted circles; sycamore wood; c. 1875; 6"; $75.00.

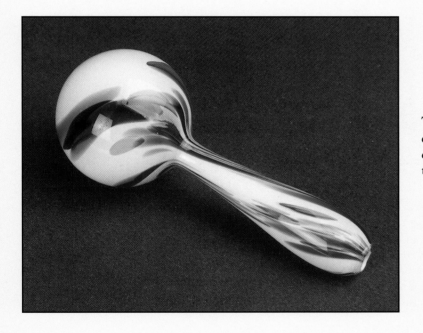

This colorful glass darner is known to some as "end of day"; open pontil; Wayne Muller in his book *Darner It!* describes one similar; small ball on handle; free blown; three layer cased; generic name "spatter glass"; $165.00.

USA; varnished wood; egg-shaped top with glove darner handle, needles in handle, thimble on finial, telescope fit, tight; US Patent 1885; 6"; $38.00.

Top row:

1, 2. USA; two sterling handled enameled child's darners, c. 1925.

    1. White; handle slightly bent; 5"; $18.00.

    2. Black; good condition; 4½"; $55.00.

3. USA; bottle glass, hand-blown open pontil, soft blue; 5"; $60.00.

4. USA; celluloid; egg darner is two pieces molded, joined perfectly with grain, handle two pieces molded to look "turned"; 7"; $58.00.

5. USA; black enameled egg, turned, natural wood handle; 6¼"; $50.00.

Row two:

1. USA, New England; solid wood egg darner, original old green paint; c. 1900; 2" x 3½"; $18.00.

2. Scotland; Stickware, Mauchline; darner ball, stained wood; $40.00.

Row three:

1. – 4. USA; sterling and wood handles, glove darners.

    1. Rope twist handle, two different sizes of small darners; 4"; $65.00.

    2. Wood, black enamel; sterling band on handle; 4⅜"; $50.00.

    3. Wood stained; darner and punch; 4½"; $14.00.

    4. Wood, light blue enamel; round rends; 4"; $10.00.

Clamps

Birds, Reel and Swift

In *An Illustrated History of Needlework Tools* Gay Ann Rogers writes "Needlework clamp has become the accepted generic term to describe the variety of fabric and thread holders which function as an extra hand to hold taut the fabric being stitched or the thread being wound. The stand of the needlework clamp is attached to the table edge not by a clamp but by a thumbscrew-operated slip-vice."

The many varieties of the "sewing bird clamps" remained popular and manufactured for nearly a hundred years. (See page 35.) The early clamps were ivory and bone and were in sewing tool boxes well into the mid-1900s. Other figural clamps such as the dolphin and butterfly; were and still are sought after. The expandable Swift made preparation of yarn for knitting easier and quicker. For fine thread, reels were used. By the mid-1800s the hemming clamp and winding clamp were necessary sewing tools making multiple projects possible with one tool. Often two clamps would be used on one project to hold hemming or seam stitching taut and secure. The clamp manufacturers diversified them by adding additional pincushions, needle holders, reels, and tape measures. Note the early iron clamp with an embroidery hoop, page 36.

Estelle Zalkin included a nineteenth century ditty in *Thimbles and Sewing Implements:*
"Behold a willing warbler
Contrived so cunningly.
The hems you turn
We'll hold quite firm
Not pinned on your knee."
Size should not discourage your search, there are small, medium, and large as well as plain and beautiful.

Portfolio of Lady Duff-Gordon's Original Designs, 1917.

1. USA; sewing bird; pressed brass upper and under body, clamp, heart-shaped thumb screw, and molded iron, note the "silver" paint, replaced pincushion; c. 1850; $120.00.
2. England; silver plate; column topped with velvet pincushion; needlecase mounted on front of the "c" clamp with acorn screw top; disc thumbscrew; c. 1855; bird 2¾", clamp 5½" high; $800.00.

1. USA; sewing bird, pressed brass wings and back; iron under body; molded iron clamp and thumbscrew; small flared emery holder; c. 1855; $110.00.
2. England; cast iron; designs hand painted on wings and back, disc thumbscrew; early 1800s; $110.00.
3. Sewing bird, pressed brass body; originally had an emery on the back, a missing pincushion under the throat; "c" clamp and thumbscrew are brass; c. 1853; $90.00.

1. England; iron dolphin sewing clamp, angel thumbscrew; c. 1870; 6" x 5½"; $1,250.00.
2. Germany; chrome-plated steel; plunger at base of cylinder on front of "c" clamp, when pushed up lifts ball up to hold fabric; spindle for thread behind fabric grip; many German clamps are behind fabric grip; many German clamps are variations of this style; c. 1900; 4" x 2½"; $105.00.
3. USA; cast-iron embroidery hoop clamp; top thumbscrew opens the hoop for securing fabric for handwork, thumbscrew just below the ball joint releases the joint for positioning the ring, lower thumbscrew tightens clamp to work area such as a table, chair, work box; c. 1850; 8½" x 5"; $100.00.

England; Georgian; sewing clamp, beautiful wood work, velvet pincushion; spring drawer for storage; wood thumbscrew with ivory finial; c. 1820; $450.00.

1. China; ivory clamp, made for lacemaking boxes; replaced pincushion; c. 1810 – 1850; $100.00.
2. England; ivory clamp with beautiful carved design thumbscrew, slightly chipped; velvet pincushion cup mounted on column; c. 1840; $350.00.
3. China; ivory clamp, thread "catcher" atop column; small pincushion; painted carved circles; c. 1810 – 1850; $275.00.

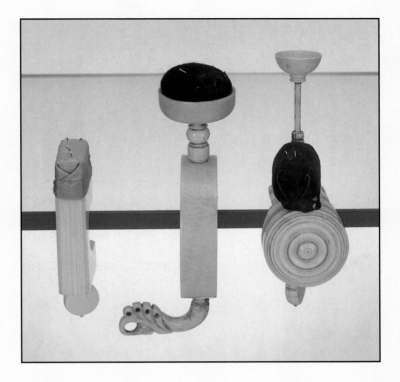

1. England, ebony, mother-of-pearl inlay cushion cup and clamp; velvet pincushion, indented thumbscrew; c. 1820; 5"; $350.00.
2. England; Mauchline; wood, carved out painted circles, tape measure cylinder mounted on front of clamp, paper label "A Brighton Gift," released and returned by hand; souvenir; replaced pincushion; c. 1800; 2½"; $225.00.

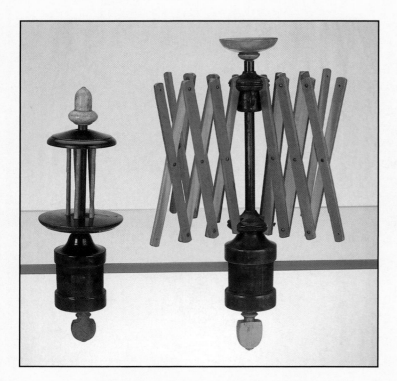

1. England; winding clamp, holly and mahogany wood; used in pairs for linen and yarn; c. 1860; 10"; $210.00.
2. England; mahogany and holly wood swift for more coarse yarns; expandable cage; the cup on top held a yarn ball; c. 1865; 10"; $250.00.

1, 3. England; Mauchline clamp, painted sycamore.
   1. Pincushion replaced, c. 1855; 4"; $150.00.
   3. Pincushion in cup; c. 1855; 6"; $150.00.
   2. England; blending Georgian and Chinoiserie designs for sewing clamp; painted scene of two women in a garden, Chinese motif; pin-cushioned lid screws on and off showing small storage area, silk cover deteriorated, batting exposed; c. 1840; 6"; $250.00.

1, 2, 4, 5. England, Tunbridge; mahogany sewing clamps, c. 1850.

    1, 4, 5. Half square mosaic-patterned veneer; rosewood; 4"; $325.00.

    2. Rosewood half-mosaic pattern of roses and leaves (stickware units dyed colors needed for pattern); original velvet pincushion in stickware cup; 5½"; $400.00.

3. USA; walnut wood, handcrafted, dove tailing on front of clamp; thumbscrew 5", has padded disc to protect table when in use; pincushion mounted on 2" post, has filigree brass band; c. 1915; $65.00.

1, 2. England; wooden painted clamps; mirror, natural-wood clamp screw handle; c. 1875.

    1. Large mirror; velvet cushion; 5½"; $80.00.

    2. Small mirror; replaced cushion; 7"; $65.00.

1. Germany; wood, pictorial decal, souvenir picture: "Souefo Laxenburg bei Wein"; original pincushion; c. 1875; 7"; $125.00.

2. England; Mauchline, Scotland; hand-painted floral cluster; 8½"; $170.00.

3. Austria, "Aussee"; burnt wood designs, hand painted; original pincushion; souvenir; 8½"; $125.00.

1. Germany; small metal clamp, spring action; original velvet pincushion; made for Helenor Tool and Supply Co., New York, NY; c. 1925; 2½"; $10.00.
2. USA; wood, handcrafted rectangular clamp; wool pincushion; short thumb-screw; c. 1930; 3" x 9"; $20.00.
3. North Europe; wood clamp, handmade, design to fit various table sizes; leather strap holding pincushion base together, split in wood; homespun cover of cushion; c. 1860; 10"; $20.00.
4. USA; wood sewing box with clamp sheltered underneath in recessed area; storage drawer brass pull; cotton covered pincushion; c. 1920; 4"; $18.00.
5. USA; metal, braided rug clamp, holds fabric strips, grip stops flow; diamond design on clamp; c. 1935; 4½"; $12.00.

1. England, steel sewing clamp, stylized "bird" with exaggerated tail is pushed down to open the mouth for holding fabric, four hand-turned wood reels for thread; "cup" filled with emery acts as pincushion; c. 1780 – 1820; 2½" x 7"; $200.00.
2. USA; brass sewing bird, molded feather designs on body, decorative clamp (vice); spring action to open mouth for holding fabric; bird 1½" x 3", clamp 1" x 3½"; $175.00.

Needles & Pins, Holders & Cushions

The photograph on page 50 will be of interest to those who enjoy knowing how antique items were manufactured. It is complete with a sample of the quality packaging. The display was designed for stores that catered to the individuals that did the sewing for households and individuals. JF Milward produced needles in the late 1800s in Redditch, England, as did a number of other manufacturers.

When comparing the variety of needles available in the late 1800s, it is interesting to note that manufacturers made needles for hand sewing, embroidery, darning, tailoring, beading, upholstering, as well as for sailmaking.

Jeffrey Hopewell writes in "Pillow Lace and Bobbins" that lacemakers were using brass pins for pattern punching and pattern guides when making lace. The brass pins would not rust and were used as early as the 1500s. These pins were headless

and later heads were attached separately. In 1824 the solid head pin was invented. Glass-head brass pins came from France and were preferred for lacemaking and household sewing.

Holders were a necessity for protecting needles and pins from rusting and misplacing them, they were valuable. The Victorian Industrial Revolution mass production gave rise to an affluent middle class. Pincushions were designed for use in any room in the house. Figural pincushions were particularly popular. The subjects were children, a variety of animals that were popular household pets such as bulldogs and wire-hair terriers. They were made of precious metals, mother-of-pearl, china, carved wood, brass, iron, steel, celluloid, pot metal, and fabric. The closed holders for both needles and pins can be found made of the same materials. Both are a delight to collect but some styles and subjects have become expensive.

1897 Sears & Roebuck Catalogue, 1968.

The Best of Sears Collectibles 1905 – 1910, 1976.

Top row:
1. England; Redditch; manufacturer William Avery and Son produced unusual brass holders; the "Quadruple Gold Casket" became the most popular item, it holds four packages of needles, retrieve them by sliding the bead in curved slot toward the size needed (it is upside down, note decorative butterfly on the leaf); c. 1855; $200.00.
2. England; "Unique" rolled stamped brass, ornate designs on front and back, registered April 6, 1869; manufacturer William Lewis; four slots for needle packets; the cover has American needle manufacturer and logo on front and back "R.J. Roberts, very best, Patent Parabola, Needles"; $700.00.
3. England and Germany; nanny pins; 1 & 2 brass, gold-stone setting; 3 & 4 green stone and red stone; each one unscrews at one end and has a cylinder to hold a needle and pin, thread for repairs if children tear a garment while playing (so the story goes, they were given to the nanny of the Victorian household); $225.00 – 275.00.
4. Scotland, Mauchline transferware of an etching of "Grasmere Church Lake District," made for American markets by R.J. Roberts Needles; needle book blue lining; c. 1860; $125.00.

Row two:
1. England; unmarked/W. Avery & Son Redditch; "Sheaf of Wheat"; registered 09/14/1873, brass needle holder; $300.00.
2. England; Avery & Son Redditch/W. Whiteleys of Westbourne Grove; registered 06/23/1876; brass horseshoe needle holder; $375.00.
3. England; unmarked/H. Milward/"patent Perry & Co London" wrapped needles; registered 03/04/1867, William Lewis & George Archibold; listed under "Accordian" in *Victorian Brass Needlecases* by E. Horowitz and R. Mann; "a non-figural rectangular case that opens at the top and bottom. It contains several hinged sections, usually 4 – 6. Front and back have decorative medallion of flowers; this needle case is known to most collectors as 'The Beatrice' "; 1" x 2"; $325.00.

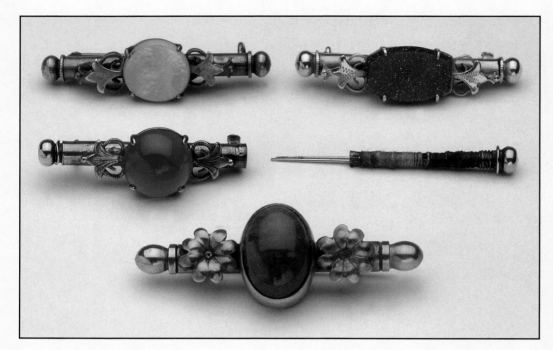

These decorative nanny brooches were also functional. Present day they are more commonly called nanny pins. These four pins are decorated with a variety of different colors of stones. The goldstone of different sizes and shapes are the most common settings of the pins we find today. Other settings were small cameos and pieces of turquoise. The center pin is open showing the cylinder for needles and thread wrapped around the cylinder, when replaced it is screwed to the hallow shaft of the pin. The pins were worn as jewelry. c. 1870; Germany and England; $190.00 – 260.00.

Top:
1. France; unusual chatelaine needle holder; beautiful imagery of a sorcerer/wizard, snake in hand; sterling; 6"; NPA.

Bottom:
2. France; sterling knitting needle guard; unscrews at three lines near center of key; decorative pair of silver chains; possibly a chatelaine piece; c. 1870; 6"; $170.00.

Top row:
1. England; bone urn-shaped needle case, pewter decorative work, mirror losing reflection; c. 1850; 1" x 2½"; $60.00.
2. England; handcarved bone, lotus leaves and grass; c. 1840; 1" x 2½"; $80.00.
3. England; ivory with gold band; c. 1860; 1½"; $40.00.
4. China; ivory; handcarved leaves; c. 1850; $75.00.
5. England; ivory tambour handle; two stanhopes, top man on horse back, middle "Columbian Expositions, 1893; Chicago, Il"; $150.00.
6. France; ivory, standing man in traditional dress, "Fisher Folk" Dieppe seaport; c. 1750; $500.00.
7. Asia; bone with brass trim; c. 1860; $25.00.
8. France; ivory, decorative carved "umbrella"; stanhope in handle with four different pictures; crochet hook at the bottom; c. 1860; 4½"; $150.00.
9. France; mother-of-pearl, two gold bands; c. 1810; 2⅞"; $100.00.
10. China; mother-of-pearl, bird and floral spray etched and painted black; c. 1850; 3"; $75.00.

Row two:
1. Egypt, Alexandria; 600 ct. silver hallmark; decorative silver cover over a stone that may have been used for sharpening pins, needles, scissors, small knives; c. 1875; $150.00.
2. USA; sterling; cap with decorative edge; c. 1930; 2½"; $45.00.
3. Flemish; .800 silver; repoussé flowers, leaves, stems; c. 1870; 4"; $150.00.
4. France; sterling; case for beading needles; c. 1860; 4"; $160.00.
5. USA; sterling; decorative leaves, cartouche; c. 1920; 2"; $35.00.
6. France; .800 silver; column, palm frons; c. 1915; 3"; $48.00.
7. USA; silver plate; leafy design; c. 1950; 2½"; $35.00.
8. Austria; silver; "A.M."; small flowers, leaves; c. 1840; 3½"; $125.00.
9. USA; sterling, Webster Co.; design of orchids; 2"; $60.00.
10. France; sterling; ribbing and loop design; c. 1900; 2¾"; $65.00.
11. England; Georgian; design of leaves, vines; c. 1840; 3"; $100.00.
12. USA; "L" mark; double beading on both sides with chain; c. 1915; 3"; $60.00.

Top row:

1. England; Victorian advertising fold-up; "Clark's ONT spool cotton," "Marshall's Linen thread," "Milward's Helix Needles"; outside "To make a beautiful little mantle screen, bend paper forward carefully on dotted lines"; title "Foreman of the Jury: Our unanimous verdict is that ONT Beats all others" MKCO; $30.00.

2 – 4. USA, England; assorted packages of Sharp needles, c.1875; $3.00 each.

5. USA; Singer sewing machine needles; Simanco TM; for treadle machines; c. 1900; $3.00.

6. England; Jas. Smith & Sons; sharps; $5.00.

7. England; John English; carpet needles; $3.00.

8. USA; J. & P. Coats metal needle threader, "Always use J. & P. Coats Boilfast will not run or stain"; back has instructions on how to use the threader and can be used to thread machines; $10.00.

Row two:

1. England; Redditch; three packages "Flora MacDonald" needles crewel, chenille, betweens made by Abel Morrall "over a century's reputation"; $12.00.

Row three:

1. England, Redditch; H. Milward & Sons; betweens size 5; c. 1857; $5.00.

2. England, Redditch; H. Milwards; sharps; "J. & P. Coats spool cotton" and "Clark spool cotton" on back; $3.00.

3. England, Redditch; large eye betweens 5/10; Coats and Clark advertising on back; $2.00.

4. England; Redditch and London; red leather fold-up needle case, gold lettering; two rows of different sizes and kinds of sewing needles; TM crossed Foxes Abel Morrall; $25.00.

5. England; Crowley's fold-up leather needle case, gold lettering; twelve sizes; $8.00.

6. England; Brabant Needle Co Ltd, Redditch; nickel-plated "Yarn Darners," size 14 – 18; $7.00.

7. Germany; Jubilee, "Best Yarn Darners," size 14 – 18; $3.00.

Row four:

1. England; Redditch; "Purse of Needles"; John James & Sons; $7.00.

2. Germany; Aix La Chapelle prize medal needles; St. Beissel, W. & Son; cloth cover; $6.00.

Needlecraft Magazine, November 1928.

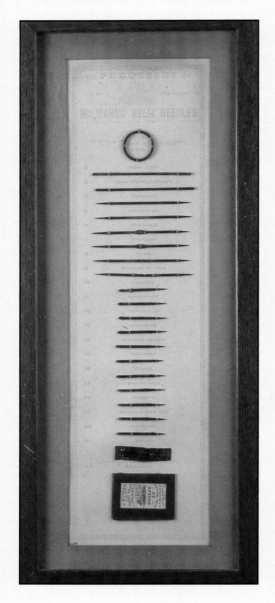

Process in the manufacture of Melrose Helix Needles

1. coil of wire	12. tempered
2. wire cut	13. crooked
3. wire straightened	14. straightened
4. pointed	15. scoured
5. skimmed	16. blued
6. pressed	17. burnished
7. pierced	18. ground
8. filed	19. ground and set
9. broken in two	20. polished
10. headed	21. stuck
11. hardened	22. papered

Commercial packaging and label
Patent wrappers, JF Milward sole agent 1887

1. England; Redditch, W. Avery/Baggallays, Westfall & Spence Des Pat 292979 07/19/1875; "Easel" holding container of three packets of needles; beautiful floral on face of the box; $290.00.
2. France; ivory "umbrella" needle case, clove "hoof" with Stanhope, screw top, lead pencil holder at tip end; Stanhope picture of Crystal Palace "made in France"; c. 1851; $110.00.

Pincushions
Figural, Decorative & Ordinary

The quality of the straight pin and availability changed with mass production in the mid-1800s. Prior to that time the pins were crude and expensive. They were used for sewing but also needed for use as fasteners of clothing. With the public's ability to purchase as many pins as needed, the role of the pincushion changed. They were no longer just one or two ordinary items for sewing purposes. The Victorian pincushion became a fashion statement along with other household decorating accessories. They were taken out of the sewing area and placed throughout the house. The filling of choice was emery because of the abrasive quality for removing rust and sharpening the points of pins and needles. Other fillings, probably because of availability for homemade cushions, were fibers of cotton, wool, and silk, as well as horse hair and saw dust. The figural pincushion became the most popular because of the diversity that became available. The bases were made of every imaginable material, from precious metals, to paper and everything in between.

The rusting of pins and needles continued to be a problem until stainless steel became available. The pin and needle cases helped minimize the problem as well as adding an attractive new sewing item to their sewing basket. The materials they were made of ranged from very ornate and expensive to simple and affordable.

Pincushions and needle holders adorned other sewing tools such as sewing clamps, thread holders, sewing boxes, chatelaines, and baskets. Collectors have a wide choice of these items in age range and styles. Just be certain of what you buy. There are more and more reproductions of sewing tools than ever. Reproductions have a real place in collecting as long as that is what you want and are not paying antiques prices.

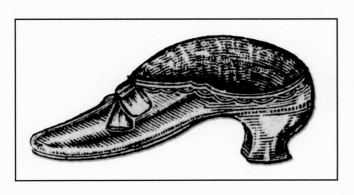

Montgomery Ward and Co. Fall & Winter Catalogue No. 56, 1894 – 95, 1970.

USA; redware pottery, bulldog pincushion; 6";
$200.00.

Top row:
1. USA; tin doll's head; fashion pincushion; blue glass eyes; painted brows, lashes, face, and hair; antique fabric and lace clothing; c. 1900; $175.00.

Row two:
1. USA; "Pan American Exposition 1937," on other side "Robert"; base metal; $40.00.
2. USA; silver pincushion holder and red covered cushion; chatelaine piece; c. 1875; $70.00.
3. Japan; "tomato" emery, star-shaped leaves; c. 1930; $12.00.

Clockwise:
1. USA; Honeysuckle reeds, woven basket with handles, filled with cotton, covered with hand crochet mesh; pink and red cotton roses attached to basket; c. 1890; 3½"; $38.00.
2. USA, New England; birch bark canoe, black velvet cushion silk "hanger"; souvenir; c. 1920; $18.00.
3. USA; felt sunflower pincushion; wool; c. 1910; $15.00.
4. USA; ribbon chatelaine, half-walnut shells form covered pincushions; c. 1930; $18.00.
5. USA, New England; simple household pill box filled with common straight pins; c. 1940; $7.00.
6. England; lady's silk boot pincushion, lace trim; c. 1875; $65.00.
7. USA; J. Bacon & Sons Mfr; cardboard pin cube, black and white glass head pins, "Toilet Pins"; c. 1900; $20.00.
8. USA; cross-stitched pincushion, beautiful handwork; glass-head pins; c. 1940; $50.00.
9. England; wood heart decorated with seashells; popular seaside souvenir when railroads made coastal areas accessible; c. 1880; $45.00.

Center:
10. USA; wood snow sled, "Queen" on one blade; c. 1900; $60.00.
11. USA; Viking pins, brass wire, 160 count, size s – c; attractive art work; c. 1920; $15.00.

England; Victorian short boot, wood, hand-painted butterflies, roses; velvet cushion; c. 1900; $75.00.

1. Germany; beautiful 4" jointed doll on stand holding a brimmed thimble holder; collection item; c. 1890; $150.00.
2. Germany; pincushion made in style of a fashion doll; head and breast plate good condition; fabric and lace of the period; c. 1890; 4" x 5½"; $200.00.
3. Germany; bisque doll; pin holder; fully jointed body, seated, mohair wig; long wool day dress, pins lined up along top of hem; lace cap silk ribbon; collection item; c. 1890; 4"; $150.00.

Top row:
1. England; open-mouth fish holding pincushion, blackened metal, on low stand; c. 1875; 2½"; $85.00.
2. England; seated dog, nickel finish pot metal; one eye and leg wrapped with a bandage, neck collar, cushion on back; c. 1900; 2½" x 3½"; $75.00.
3. England; bull dog, pot metal; green velvet cushion; c. 1890; 3" x 3¾"; $90.00.
4. Germany; bull dog seated, brown glass eyes, pot metal, black velvet cushion; c. 1900; 2¾" x 3½"; $95.00.
5. Germany; seated cat, nickel finish, neck ribbon, velvet cushion; 2½" x 3¼"; $110.00.
6. England; seated frog, head turned up holding velvet pincushion; blackened finish pot metal; $75.00.

Row two:
1. USA; gilded, seated lion; cushion on back; 2½" x 5"; $48.00.
2. Germany; swallow, nickel finish pot metal, good condition, black glass eyes, velvet cushion; c. 1900; $125.00.
3. Seated cat, pot metal, pincushion pile loss; c. 1900; 1½" x 2½"; $60.00.

Row three:
1. England; seated sheep, pot metal, damaged pincushion; c. 1900; $125.00.
2. England; seated rabbit; pot metal, velvet cushion; c. 1890; 1¾" x 4"; $150.00.

Row four:
1. England; seated cat; pot metal, worn gold pincushion; c. 1890; 1½" x 2½"; $70.00.

Top row:
1. USA; hissing cat; pot metal; worn pincushion; c. 1900; 1½" x 3"; $55.00.
2. England; cat with back arched; pot metal; 1½" x 2"; $65.00.
3. France; rooster; beautiful mold, pincushion below open grid work on the back; brass; c. 1870; 3¾"; $110.00.
4. England; bull dog seated; nickel finish pot metal; 2½" x 3½"; $55.00.
5. USA; "migrating" buffalo; pot metal, velvet cushion; c. 1900; 2" x 3"; $90.00.

Row two:
1. Germany; bull dog, brown glass eyes; velvet cushion; c. 1900; 1¾" x 3"; $95.00.
2. USA; pig, nickel finish pot metal, stripe pincushion; #155; 1¾" x 2¾"; $50.00.
3. England; seated cat, neck ribbon and bow; c. 1875; $55.00.
4. Elephant standing with outstretched trunk; worn gilt finish; "ANCO 2176"; c. 1900; 1½" x 3"; $60.00.
5. Flacon, at rest; worn gilt finish, pot metal; c. 1900; 1¼" x 3"; $45.00.

Row three:
1. Pig standing, pot metal, velvet cushion; $70.00.
2. Germany; gilded swan, pot metal, red velvet cushion; 1¾" x 2¼"; $45.00.
3. Germany; swan, nickel plated pot metal, velvet cushion; $45.00.
4. Gilded seated pig; green velvet cushion; 1½" x 2"; $48.00.

Row four:
1. England; cat standing on hind legs rolling brass tape measure ball (tape missing), brass tail winder for original tape; "MS22172" stamp; c. 1860; 1½" x 2"; $50.00.
2. USA; miniature silver duck; velvet cushion, ½" x 1¼"; reproduction 1990; $48.00.

55

Page 57 shows *the* shoe photo. The time frame is 1840 to 1940 and includes work shoes, dress shoes, and a boot or two made of wood, silver, base metal; hand carved and molded. Small models of ladies' dress shoes, historic and contemporary, are being reproduced. They have captured the collectors' interest. These in the book are all pincushions that were ornamental as well as functional in Victorian to Depression era homes. The women not only displayed them with pride throughout their homes, but also adorned the cushion with an array of pins and needles.

Top row:
1. USA; pot metal unlaced boot with velvet cushion; c. 1880; 2¼"; $75.00.
2. Central Europe; wood, pointed toe shoe, decorative cross hatch and diamond design; replaced cushion, hand carved; c. 1900; 2" x 4½"; $35.00.
3. USA; wood man's boot, unlaced, small braid laces, handcrafted; hole in side of boot; signed "OH 1917 W"; 2½" x 3½"; $45.00.
4. USA; lady's dress shoe; nickel finish pot metal; medallion buckle, velour cushion; c. 1875; 1½" x 5"; $40.00.
5 & 6. England; pair of men's dress shoes; nickel-plated pot metal; velour covered cushion; c. 1880; 2½" x 4"; $125.00.

Row two:
1. USA; wood, lady's half boot, hand carved; eyelets, no lacings; c. 1875; 2" x 2¼"; $50.00.
2 & 3. USA; pair of lady's dress pumps, wood; decorative glass bead "buckle"; velour cushions; c. 1940; 2" x 3"; $25.00.
4. England; lady's walking shoe; pewter; velvet cushion; c. 1880; 1½" x 2¼"; $50.00.
5. England, Sheffield; nickel-plated pot metal man's dress shoe, spats & buttons; velvet cushion; c. 1880; 2" x 3½"; $60.00.
6. Scandinavian; slipper, brass; punctured markings; velvet cushion; c. 1870; 1½" x 3¼"; $48.00.

Row three:
1. England; man's shoe, hand-carved wood, sole "splitting" from toe depicting hard times; c. 1900; 1¼" x 2½"; $52.00.
2. Holland; stylized shoe; nickel finish pot metal; decorative figures in traditional dress; tulips, windmill; souvenir; c. 1840 style, made c. 1890; $40.00.
3. USA; silver-plated lady's dress shoe; blue velvet cushion; c. 1915; 2" x 4"; $55.00.
4. USA; lady's dress shoe, bronze finish pot metal; floral buckle; worn orange velvet cushion; c. 1900; $75.00.
5. England; lady's dress shoe, brass; low heel; ribbon lacings; velvet cushion; c. 1875; ½" x 3"; $85.00.

Montgomery Ward & Co., Fall & Winter Catalogue No. 56, 1894 – 95.

Montgomery Ward & Co., Fall & Winter Catalogue No. 56, 1894 – 95.

Top row:
1. England; man's shoe, hand-carved sycamore, worn velvet cushion; c. 1875; 1¼" x 3¼"; $65.00.
2. Ireland; three-legged pot, two handles, decorative carved shamrocks; bog oak; c. 1900; 1½" x 3¼"; $75.00.
3. Asia; hand-carved ivory, double pincushions on footed post; c. 1860; 3" x 3"; $150.00.
4. England; wood; covered pincushion; hand-painted sprays of roses on screw top; light blue silk cushion; c. 1875; 1¼" x 2"; $55.00.
5. Japan; lavender celluloid slipper, one of a pair; machine blanket stitch; c. 1920; 1½" x 3"; $10.00.

Row two:
1. Asia; hand-carved vegetable ivory; scalloped edge; low stand; European export; c. 1860; 1½" x 1"; $35.00.
2. China; heavily carved bone; cushion holder on screw stand; cotton cushion; c. 1865; 1½" x 1"; $30.00.
3. China; vegetable ivory; open work carving; c. 1860; 1" x 1¾"; $45.00.
4. China; ivory crown style holder; c. 1860; 1" x 1¼"; $50.00.
5. China; vegetable ivory; lotus blossom design holder; low stand; c. 1860; 1" x 1⅜"; $70.00.

Row three:
1. USA; wood pinkeep; orange velvet cushion; c. 1890; 2¼" x ⅝"; $25.00.
2. China; vegetable ivory shaped like a rice farmer's hat on both sides of pinkeep; c. 1860; $45.00.
3. Jerusalem; olive wood pinkeep; souvenir; ½" x 2"; c. 1960; $45.00.
4. England; carved ivory lady's dress shoe; blue silk cushion; c. 1840; ¼" x 2"; $100.00.

Top row:
1. USA; glass candlestick base, make-do pincushion, crazy patch covered cushion; c. 1890; 3½" x 4½"; $35.00.
2. USA, Ohio; glass compote stand, make-do pincushion; simple crazy patch cushion cover and soutache fringe; c. 1900; 3" x 4½"; $32.00.
3. USA, Spartanburg, South Carolina; wood pincushion chair on base with drawer; hand carved and upholstered, mahogany stain; from Bon Haven, a home on the National Registry; it was the Cleveland home on N. Church St., Spartanburg, SC; c. 1850; 3½" x 7½" x 9"; $200.00.
4. USA; Northern Ohio; hand carved from one piece of wood by famous family of small and large wooden household items; velvet pincushion; c. 1910; $55.00.
5. USA; Art Nouveau style vanity box; gray velvet cushion and silver grill, curves, and flowers; mfg. James Wooley, Boston; c. 1900; 5" x 2¼"; $78.00.

Row two:
1. England; cast-iron urn pincushion, scalloped edge; tan velvet cushion; c. 1860; 3½" x 4"; $78.00.
2, 4. Scotland; tartan souvenir, bagpipe, ruffled pincushion in original boxes; embroidery "Frae Scotland," "Frae Bonnie Scotland"; c. 1970; $15.00 each.
3. England; Wm Avery & Son, Redditch; brass walnut on leaf stand for short needles such as betweens; hinged top; registered 05/08/1873; 2¾" x 3"; $500.00.
5. England; partridge, seated; pot metal; c. 1880; 3"; $65.00.
6. USA, New England; pin roll, wool with embroidery, fringe; c. 1890; 5"; $50.00.

Top row:

1. Japan; cotton covered tomato pincushion, small matching emery and label; c. 1920; 1" x 2½"; $7.00.

2 – 9. USA; plain and fancy emeries used for sharpening points of needles, removing rust; they are found in sewing baskets, boxes, and attached to chatelaines, treadle machine drawers are often a treasure trove of small sewing items including emeries; these emeries are from 1" to 2" in length; 2, 3, 4 have appliqué felt leaves; two cotton covers one velvet, silk, and beautiful bead work; c. 1880 – 1920; $4.00 – 55.00 each.

    5 – 9. Emeries have hand-embroidered leaves (caps); handmade strawberries; 5 has beautiful silk fabric and thread; $5.00 – 25.00 each.

Row two:

1. England; beaded hexagon pinkeep; six-pointed star design with glass beads of red, white, and green in center and other side cornucopia of flowers; red, orange, white, green, and blue; cushion fill covered with silk fabric; c. 1890; 2" x 2"; $48.00.

2. USA, New England; Native American sweet grass basket; pincushion, silk thread dividers; c. 1920; 1" x 2"; $25.00.

3. Scotland; heart-shaped tartan pinkeep; souvenir, "Frae Bonnie Scotland"; 5"; $35.00.

4. China; decorative carved mother-of-pearl pinkeep; handmade; new silk cover; c. 1860; $65.00.

5. USA; heart-shaped pinkeep; painted silk of daisies and leaves; velvet cushion cover; c. 1900; $18.00.

Row three:

1. USA; pinkeep with beautiful wheel of blue enamel and sterling silver on both sides; marked "F & B Sterling 112"; $100.00.

2. USA; heart-shaped pincushion; handmade; paisley fabric, braid trim, some fraying; c. 1910; 2" x 2½"; $15.00.

3. England; doubled end wood pincushion, barrel shape; blue silk covers; c. 1875; 1½"; $30.00.

4. England; sterling silver cover HM "Birmingham, 1908," "L & S"; $75.00.

5. USA; handmade and beaded pincushion "gift for friend"; circle of flowers, orange beads; some wear; c. 1900; $10.00.

Row four:

1. USA; round handmade pincushion; silk with leather overlay, silk thread trim; c. 1900; 1¼"; $30.00.

2 – 3. China; mother-of-pearl lacemaking box tools; c. 1860; $100.00 pair.

    2. Thread waxer.

    3. Pinkeep, silk cover.

4. USA; leather-covered brocade pincushion; some wear; c. 1890; 1½"; $10.00.

Top row:
1. USA; portmanteau pincushion, gilded; c. 1920; $20.00.
2. USA, Massachusetts; Pilgrim cradle, pincushion; stamped "Pat. Apl. for EDES MFG. Co., Plymouth, MA"; specific style with hood and rockers; c. 1840; 1¾" x 4½"; NPA.
3. England; brass pincushion; traditional clothing for Dutch boys; 3½" x 4"; $10.00.
4. Germany, Black Forest; sitting bear hugging a navy blue pincushion; glass eyes; c. 1890; 3" x 3"; $225.00.

Row two:
1. Japan; glazed plaster pincushion; Dutch girl reading a book, flower pot holding cushion; c. 1930; 2½" x 3"; $22.00.
2. Germany; nickel-finished helmet; two pincushions, one on each side, brown velvet; c 1860; 3" x 3"; $100.00.
3. USA; "Washington DC, the Capitol"; hexagon container with pincushion; c. 1915; 2" x 2"; $18.00.
4. USA; glazed plaster shoe pincushion; cat watching the mouse come out of the toe of the shoe; c. 1920; 2" x 4"; $15.00.

Row three:
1. Middle East; brass pincushion; small man wearing turban, carrying large cushioned basket; c. 1920; 1½" x 2"; $20.00.
2. USA; gilded pot metal "piano" pincushion; souvenir of "San Francisco"; c. 1930; 2" x 2" x ½"; $15.00.
3. England; Humpty Dumpty polished pot metal pincushion; 1½" x 2"; $45.00.

Top row:
1. Germany; wrist pincushion, expandable band; stamped "Helenor Tools & Supply Co., New York: made in Germany"; velvet cushion filled with sawdust; c. 1940; 2½" x 4"; $7.00.
2. New Hampshire; make-do pincushion, stem of wine glass holding velour eggplant; marked Fry '99; 3½" x 10½"; $25.00.
3. France; sewing box with pincushion on the top; box is a Victorian molded design, silk lining with tools, sterling needle case, thimble, and punch, steel scissors; made for the public that could not afford a Palais Royal sewing box; $125.00.

Row two:
1. USA; handmade designer strawberry pincushion; velvet, appliqué leaves decorated with pearls; c. 1910; 3½" x 4¼"; $40.00.

Top row:
1. France; child standing on straight pin box; Bakelite; c. 1920; 2"; $50.00.
2. England; Bakelite pig pincushion; c. 1920; $85.00.
3. Germany; the blackberry pin case, 40 pins; rolled paper holder; glass head pins; horseshoe trademark; c. 1900; ¾" x 2"; $20.00.
4. Germany; berry case containing 40 best steel pins with glass heads; "Registered Dragon Trademark"; c. 1900; ½" x 3"; $15.00.
5. Middle East; architectural pincushion; c. 1900; 1½" x 2"; $85.00.

Row two:
1. USA; a pair of "ears of corn" pin holders; corn silk synthetic thread; kernels pearl head pins; shucks velvet; 1" x 5½"; $50.00 pair.

Row three:
1. Germany; advertising paper pinkeep; boy dancing in a top hat with a cane, color; c. 1860; 1½" x 3"; $30.00.
2 – 4. USA, Newark, NJ; Prudential Ins.
    2. Prudential Girl; 1916; $30.00.
    3. Mother and baby; 1920; $25.00.
    4. Mother and child; 1930; $25.00.
5. Germany; pinkeep; drawing of girl ice skating and boys playing; color; business label on back "Art. 1009, the US leading pin block, "Seuse Brothers" (A.B. Ruemont) Aix-la-Chapella Germany"; c. 1890; $25.00.

Top row:
1. Japan; elephant, green glaze; "made in Occupied Japan"; c. 1949; 3½" x 5"; $25.00.
2. Japan; spotted donkey luster ware; c. 1920; 3½" x 4¼"; $27.00.
3. Japan; "cat and a fiddle" luster ware; marked "Made in Japan"; c. 1920; 2½" x 3"; $30.00.
4. Japan; crane in garden scene luster ware; c. 1920; 3" x 4"; $35.00.
5. Japan; lion luster ware; stamped "made in Japan"; c. 1930; $20.00.

Row two:
1. USA; blown glass three-legged turtle; yellow cushion; c. 1940; 1¼" x 3"; $10.00.
2. Japan; cat and flower pincushion, luster ware; "made in Japan"; c. 1930; 2½" x 3"; $20.00.
3. Japan; lop-eared dog luster ware; "made in Japan"; c. 1930; 2½" x 3¼"; $32.00.
4. USA; baker, glazed china; c. 1930; 2 " x 2¼"; $30.00.
5. Japan; elephant with orange ears, luster ware; $25.00.

Row three:
1. Germany; pincushion with thread and terrier ornament; c. 1920; ¾" x 3"; $30.00.
2. USA; large pincushion, cross-stitch edge and wire hair terrier, lace ruffle; silk cushion; c. 1940; 5" x 6"; $30.00.

1. USA; emery bag; silk embroidery rose, silk ribbon hanger; drawing on box top of lady sewing, watchful parrot; "Temper no smoother than her needle Which is rusty — Poor cross-patch Mag! She wouldn't dream of smiling — Tho' All she needs is an 'Emery' bag."; c. 1920; $48.00.

2. USA; celluloid doll face on front of emery cushion; wrapped with silk ribbon and bow; "Miss Dottie Demple Emery has come to visit you and keep your needle polished bright and o-o-o just as good as new"; c. 1920; $80.00.

USA, New England; Three delightful pincushion dolls; two girls and one boy; wire body frame wrapped with batting; embroidered faces; handmade accessories; 3 for $125.00.

Left to right:
1. Strawberry head; embroidered face near point of strawberry; floral print dress, fruit basket, leaf felt topknot and collar, umbrella and shoes match; c. 1930; 10½".
2. Apple head "Teresa"; flower print dress; felt leaf on head, pin shoes; butterfly net, holding blue felt butterfly; 9".
3. Onion head; two-piece suit; red silk neck tie; red shoes; carrying bouquet of flowers and walking stick; 9½". Background fabric designed by Mary Ellen Hopkins.

Germany & USA; make-do china doll head pin-cushion; velvet covered cap and cloak; head and breast plate in excellent condition; c. 1900; 8½"; $200.00.

Germany; blue silk cap and cushion cover with ruffle, from the wear of the cushion it has been for needles and pins but originally it may have been a boudoir doll for decorating a bed, popular in the 20s and 30s; "Leonora," china head and breast plate in excellent condition, spider eyes, mouth closed, mohair wig; c. 1930; 8"; $180.00.

Top row:
1. USA; small round cushion with red, black, white beading; c. 1910; $10.00.
2. USA, Kentucky; silk "pillow" pincushion; decorative groupings of glass-head pins; c. 1920; $15.00.
3. USA; designer strawberry emery, two colors of velvet, silk ribbon; handmade; c. 1920; $35.00.

Row two:
1, 3. USA; handmade; velvet; c. 1940; $12.00 each.
2. England; small strawberry emery, sterling cap; 1900; $55.00.

Row three:
1. USA; handmade strawberry emery, velvet cap glass beads outlining; c. 1900; $75.00.
2. Endland; emery filled pincushion, silk thread dividers; sterling four arm cap; c. 1880; $68.00.
3. USA; handmade; neck ribbon heart-shaped pinkeeps; grosgrain ribbon; decorative embroidery; c. 1940; $35.00.

Row four:
1. England, Birmingham; sterling handle and cap, strawberry emery; 1890; $80.00.
2. USA, Pennsylvania; four silk, embroidered heart pincushions joined with metallic thread; embroidery on both sides; c. 1900; $50.00.

Top row:
1. USA; cube pin box; gilded and marbleized paper cover; 2¼"; $22.00.
2. USA; pincushion decorated with French style glass bead work, needle pages under top; embossed silk fabric; 3" x 4"; c. 1890; $65.00.
3. USA; Native American, Northern Plains; pincushion bird glass beads, amber, brown, green; date under tail "1908" in beading; 4½" x 8"; $65.00.

Row two:
1. England; pinball knitted cover and sterling ring and chain; two geometric star patterns, green and tan; monogram "BG"; 2" x 3¼", c. 1810; $210.00.
2. USA; "Toilet Pins," black glass shade; $12.00
3. USA; pinkeep, jack of clubs card, front and back covered with fabric; 1½" x 1¾"; c. 1930; $30.00.

The Best of Sears Collectibles 1905 – 1910, 1976.

Sears, Roebuck and Co. Consumers Guide, Fall 1900, 1970.

Thimbles & Holders

The thimble as a collector item continues to stimulate the pleasure of seeking and finding. They have been an important part of the sewing basket for centuries. The earliest were from Germany. The pitted surface of the early metal thimbles made stitching easier. It is possible to find thimbles dating back from the thirteenth to seventeenth centuries made of bronze and brass. The Industrial Revolution and the rise of an affluent middle class created a much larger market for quality sewing items such as sterling and gold thimbles.

Each country sized their thimbles and marked sterling and gold carat differently. United States thimble companies' sizes were a little different from each other. Thimbles were not marked with a size before the 1800s, and were not marked for gold and silver before 1900. If a thimble is marked Sterling, the Stamping Act of 1906 requires that it contains 925 parts of silver out of 1000. The English mark for sterling is a lion. The English Hallmark includes a city of manufacture symbol and alphabet letter for date of manufacture.

There are a number of publications available now with excellent information about the history and identification of thimbles, antique and contemporary. Pursue your collecting with patience and knowledge, and keep a journal with as much information as is available on each item.

Illustration from *The Mary Frances Sewing Book* by Jane Eayre Fryer.

Montgomery Ward & Co. Fall & Winter Catalogue No. 56, 1894 – 95.

France; Palais Royal thimble handcrafted out of mother-of-pearl, note the enamel medallion pansy with a gold band, also two gold bands on the lower area; made as early as the middle ages in the Far East and Europe with plain and decorative styles; given representing social status or an expression of affection; often found as a set in Palais Royal Boxes and étuis; c. 1800 – 1825; $650.00.

1927 Edition of The Sears, Roebuck Catalogue, 1970.

Top row:
1. England; hallmark stamp "sterling, Chester, 1907" on the band; waffle design on sides; $35.00.
2. England; hallmark "Sheffield, sterling, 1978," three small decorative bands; rolled rim; $32.00.
3. England, "Sterling, Chester, 1918"; CH 5; $30.00.
4. USA; sterling; wide band "wave" design; $20.00.
5. England; "Dreema," steel lining between two layers of "solid" silver; "H.G. & S"; $35.00.

Row two:
1. USA; sterling; advertising "Chalmers Pearls" buttons, high quality mother-of-pearl; hand-out with button purchases; c. 1930; $15.00.
2. Germany; sterling; Thimble Club International "2000" wide oxidized band with flowers, and a thimble; flat cap small TCI lettering; limited edition; designer Thorvald Greif; $45.00.
3. England; sterling, Birmingham, 1953; ornate band "E.R. II Coronation 1953" souvenir; Queen's horse-drawn coach pictured on band; $350.00.
4. England; Dorcas stamped "Rd 127211 Pat 8" "sterling silver" on band; patent date 1898; steel core with silver coating; manufactured by Charles Horner; $48.00.

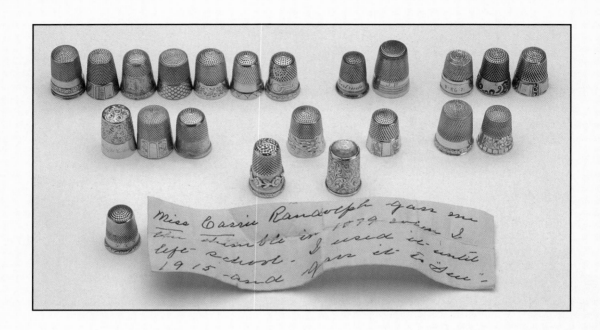

Top row:
1. USA; Simons Bros Co., Philadelphia, Pa; 10k gold; two plain and one decorative band, beaded rim; "1928," size 9; $98.00.
2. Unknown; 10k gold; decorative and plain band panels; size 6; $80.00.
3. European; 10k gold; large band with castle scenes "M.W.B."; rolled decorative rim; size 8; $75.00.
4. Unknown; 14k gold; "clam shell" design band, cartouche "A.N.F."; size 10; $150.00.
5. Unknown, wide band with floral bright work "'54 – '83" (1854 – 1883); $125.00.
6. Unknown; 10k gold; plain band, decorative rim; "H.B.L." monogram; $75.00.
7. Unknown; 10k gold; circle and bar band design; repaired; $50.00.
8. Gold fill; plain band, "Gertrude"; size 6; $35.00.
9. Germany; Gabler Bros., Schorndorf; gold fill; concentric band design, "J.P."; size 10; $35.00.
10. USA; Simons Bros., Philadelphia, PA; gold; "MMK," "5-26-71"; size 8; $65.00.
11. USA; Ketcham & McDougall, New York, NY, 1832 – 1932; sterling cap and side, 14k gold decorative band, cartouche; size 6; $80.00.
12. USA; H. Muhr & Sons, Philadelphia, PA; sterling cap and side, 14k gold band, parallel designs; "J.M.C."; repaired; $45.00.

Row two:
1. Unknown; 14k gold; heavy circular design; plain band, "Mary U. Githens"; small hole in top; $85.00.
2. Unknown; 10k gold; eleven paneled band, six leaf design, five plain; $100.00.
3. Unknown; 10k gold; plain band; size 8; $60.00.
4. USA; Ketcham & McDougall; 14k gold; slightly flared band, repoussé roses, leaves; c. 1895; $125.00.
5. USA; Carter, Gough, & Co., New York, NY; 14k gold; beveled band, five plain, six historic castle scenes, "S"; c. 1900; size 10; $120.00.
6. USA; Waite, Thresher Co; 10k gold; floral rim; c. 1907; size 11; $75.00.
7. USA; Waite, Thresher Co; 14k gold; decorative band of flowers and edge of squares; size 6; $140.00.

Row three:
1. France; two colors of gold, garland band, light, decorative rim; French applied cap separately rather than a single mold; "L" monogram; $550.00.
2. Scandinavian; 14k gold, amber stone cap; straight sides with decorative leaf design; c. 1908; size 6; $180.00.

Row four:
1. USA; 10k gold; "P.L.G."; small note rolled up in thimble: "Miss Carrie Randolph gave me this thimble in 1875 when I left school. I used it until 1915 and I gave it to Sue."; $85.00.

These thimbles are all made by Simons & Co of the United States. They are sterling and 14k gold. Simons is the only American thimble manufacturer still in business as of 2001. They did not usually give names to their designs. Gay Ann Rogers writes that European thimble manufacturers tried to increase the variety and designs of their thimbles. Use of the sterling mark began in 1857 and American manufacturers' trademarks were inside the cap.

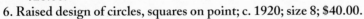

Top row:

1 – 6 Sterling

1. Interlocking chain of leaves on band; elongated hexagon design rim; size 10; $42.00.
2. Wide band of plain and small decorated panels, size 10; $38.00.
3. Beautiful wide band with grapes, vines, leaf repoussé, a cartouche; size 13; $245.00.
4. Wide bright work of leaves and flowers; size 8; $48.00.
5. Two bands, one paneled with plain and decorated units; size 10; $28.00.
6. Raised design of circles, squares on point; c. 1920; size 8; $40.00.

Row two:

1 – 6 Sterling

1. Band of concentric circles; crosshatching on sides; "Sr. C.C."; size 10; $50.00.
2. Two bands, one plain, one decorated with partial circles and center indented; size 9; $30.00.
3. Wide band, "A Stitch in Time Saves Nine"; size 8; $800.00.
4. Wide border with roses, leaves, and vines; size 11; $30.00.
5. Two borders, one plain, one Greek key; 1950; size 9; $30.00.
6. Plain band, very small fan design above rim; $15.00.

7. 14k gold; beautiful lake scene, flowers on band; scroll rim; $115.00.

Row three:

1 – 6. 14k gold

1. Plain wide band; "Mildred"; size 9; $170.00.
2. Country scene, small floral panels, cartouche "Dell" on wide band; size 9; $120.00.
3. Raised band, mounted fleur de lis on band, ring for chain mounted on the cap; NPA.
4. Two bands, one plain, other a chain design; a beveled rim; size 10; $75.00.
5. English-style rolled rim; plain band; size 9; $110.00.
6. Concentric circles on wide band; cartouche "ESC"; size 9 (similar design as #1 row two in sterling); $115.00.

Row four:

1 – 3. 14k gold

1. Floral band with decorative rim; cartouche "CR"; $100.00.
2. Beautiful jagged bright work band; size 6; $110.00.
3. Full carat mark; twelve panel band; "ALB"; size 10; $95.00.

Top row:

1 – 4. Italy; .800; ornate gilded band; semi-precious stones.

    1. Lapis lazuli, beautiful blue; $98.00.

    2. Turquoise; $98.00.

    3, 4. Persian turquoise; $100.00.

5. Opals; scalloped rim; size 10; $110.00.

6. Germany; .830 silver; royal blue enamel band with rose; red stone cap; maker Soergel and Stollmeyer 1890; $95.00.

7. Switzerland; .830 silver; blue enamel with flower garland; green stone cap; silver rim; $100.00.

8, 9, 10. Norway; enamel over sterling, moonstone cap, winter scene, child on sled pulled by reindeer; $125.00.

    9. White enamel over .925 silver; $98.00.

    10. Enamel over sterling with decorative roses on white background; cap with waffle design; "D.A." "2"; $110.00.

11. Russia; .813 silver; black lettering, waffle design cap; c. 1950; $50.00.

Row two:

1. Austrian-Hungarian; .813 silver, moonstone cap, shield cartouche, decorative band; c. 1950; size 18;

2. Israel; sterling; raised medallion, green stone, four decorative rings; thin rolled rim;

3. England; sterling; plain band; $45.00.

4. Mexico; Taxco sterling; $30.00.

5. Scandinavian; blue stone cap, repoussé roses near rim; $50.00.

6. England; .800; bright cut design rim; $45.00.

7. Italy; sterling, moonstones mounted on band; $85.00.

8, 11, 12. Germany; .800; stones mounted on band; $85.00 – 95.00.

    8. Green stone cap, turquoise mountings.

    11. Dark red mountings.

    12. Lapis mountings.

9. Italy; .800; red stone cap, plain band; $75.00.

10. Italy; .800; green stone, plain band; $80.00.

Row three:

1. England; sterling; wide band, delicate design and forget me not; 1858; $65.00.

2. Scotland; sterling; wide band with two rows berries and "Dina Forget"; 1850; $110.00.

3. England; sterling; B'ham, 1898 HM; Blackberries and leaves; $55.00

4. England, sterling; daisy design; "Blackpool" diamond band, HM; 1930; $58.00.

5. England; sterling; HM; "To Auntie from Glynis" on band; beveled edge; 1957; $45.00.

6. England; sterling, steel cap; small designs on band; c. 1820; $80.00.

7. England; sterling; alternating geometric and plain panels; 1850; $60.00.

8. Germany; sterling; heart cartouche on band; $48.00.

9. France, touchmark minimum .800; raised roses, pair of birds on band, both sides of band outlined with beading; $55.00.

10. France; hallmark .800; decorative band of heart wreath, shells, floral; $50.00.

11. Germany; mark on top .800 depose; fleur de lis on band; $48.00.

1897 Sears Roebuck Catalogue, 1968.

Top row:

1 – 3. USA; Webster Co; sterling.

    1. Dogwood branches repoussé; $70.00.

    2. Basketweave; three bands daisy chain; narrow size 9; $31.00.

    3. Daisy chain between plain bands; size 9; $32.00.

    4. England; sterling; steel cap; two small decorative bands, one plain, rolled rim; c. 1840; size 7; $35.00.

5 – 7. USA; sterling.

    5. Monogram "M.L.G."; c. 1920; size 6; $20.00.

    6. Flared rim; size 9; $22.00.

    7. "Columbian World Exposition 1892" worn; size 11; $120.00.

8. Unknown; silver plate; "Sue" on plain band; rolled rim; c. 1925; size 9; $20.00.

9. USA, NY, Weinburg Co; stamped on plain band "Nickel silver, Sterling silver, silver plated"; c. 1918; size 8; $20.00.

10. USA; Simons Co; silver fill; butterfly & flower on large band; c. 1980; $30.00.

Row two:

1. USA; Mass., Shepard Mfg. Co; band with palm frons; $70.00.

2 – 4. USA; Stern Bros.; sterling.

    2. Large band, cartouche, etched wavy lines; c. 1908; size 10; $34.00.

    3. Stern and Goldsmith, trademark stamped on band; $40.00.

    4. Stern Bros.; decorative feathers on band; size 11; $35.00.

5 – 9. USA; Providence, RI, Waite Thresher; sterling.

    5. Wide band, bright cut decorative leaves; c. 1900; size 8; $38.00.

    6. Wide decorative band; size 10; $40.00.

    7. Two sizes of beading on band; c. 1910; $32.00.

    8. Band of ten geometric designed panels; size 11; $47.00.

    9. Decorative band design of flowers and feathers; $49.00.

Row three:

1. Unknown; .800 silver; stylized flowers on band; $28.00.

2 – 7. USA; Ketcham McDougall, NY; sterling.

    2. Decorative rose branches on band; size 8; $70.00.

    3. Band with palms, beaded rim; size 6; $38.00.

    4. Wide plain band; size 6; $49.00.

    5. Rolled rim; size 8; $25.00.

    6. Monogram "F.O."; decorative, rolled rim; size 7; $25.00.

    7. Band of decorative palm frons; beaded rim; "ML"; $50.00.

8. USA; Philadelphia, PA, H. Muhr's Sons; horizontal geometric designs on band; size 7; $60.00.

Montgomery Ward & Co. Fall & Winter Catalogue No. 56, 1894 – 95.

75

The "Dorcas" thimble was designed and manufactured by Charles Horner of Great Britain by 1884. It had a steel core and silver coating. These thimbles had added strength as well as comfort for the sewer. With a quality product and merchandising skills, Charles Horner became the leading manufacturer of thimbles. The black plastic Dorcas thimble display is a late twentieth century item enjoyed by collectors. It holds 12 thimbles.

Top row:
"Dorcas"; "Pat. 10"; decorative leaf design on band; $50.00.

Row two:
1. "Daisy"; stamped "CH 9 Dorcas"; "9" was size, daisy pattern with centers, rolled rim; $50.00.
2. Bright work band of flowers; stamped "H.M. Sterling, Chester, 1890"; rolled rim; $60.00.

Row three:
1. Basketweave; stamped "HM Sterling, Chester, 1909"; $40.00.
2. Stamped "HG & S tc, 13, Dreema"; plain; $40.00.

Row four:
Dorcas; $45.00 – 75.00.
1. Stamped "Little Dreema" CH 8; daisy-like pattern overall; early.
2. Stamped "Rd 127211 Pat. 11"; daisy; c. 1905.
3. Stamped "Dreema HG & S 15"; daisy band; c. 1900.
4. Stamped "Pat. M Dorcas" 1, daisy pattern.
5. Stamped "Doris 10" "Dorcas," daisy pattern.
6. Stamped "Pat. 10" "Dorcas," star pattern.
7. Stamped "CH 9 Dorcas"; shell pattern, Rd 210799.
8. Stamped "London Dorcas 5"; rare; plain.

The children looked here and there.

They looked under this, and

they looked under that.

Susan said, "Oh, Sally.

We have looked and looked.

But we can not find it."

Sally laughed and laughed.

"Here it is!" she said.

"It is on something."

Fun with Dick and Jane, by Willian S. Gray and Mary Hill Arbuthnot, 1st edition, published 1946.

Top row:
1. USA; Simons, SBC; alloy-nickel, copper & zinc; narrow decorative band near rim; $7.50.
2. USA; aluminum whistle, red band; "See Philco Co New inventions, new circuits, music on a beam of light" Patent, B & B; $35.00.
3. USA; political hand-out, plastic, Clinton; $10.00.
4. USA; gilt over steel, Mt. Vernon; applied medallion; souvenir; 1977; $10.00.
5. USA; rolled brass; $5.00.

6. USA; Simons, SBC, alloy; decorative band; size 10; $7.50.
7. USA; polished steel, souvenir, Uncle Sam hat medallion, 1976; $12.00.
8. USA; brass, advertisement "the Prudential"; hole in top; $3.00.
9. USA; plastic, advertisement hand-out, "Singer Sewing Machine"; $10.00.
10. USA; steel; decorative band, size 12; $8.00.
11. USA; Simons see numbers 1 & 6; decorative band; $7.50.
12. Japan; wide band, rolled rim made for export; size 11; $5.00.
13. USA; aluminum, advertisement; "Table Bell Flour"; $3.00.

Row two:
1. Spain, Granada; worn enamel, gilt and silver; souvenir; $5.00.
2. Germany; brass, amethyst cap; bent; $9.00.
3. England; brass, plain band; size 3; $5.00.
4. England; brass, plain, rolled rim; stamped "England"; size 4; $12.00.
5. England; brass, "Remember Me" & flowers on band; $15.00.
6. England; heavy steel, plain band; $7.00.
7. England; aluminum; "Stratomic, England"; size 11; $7.00.
8. England; brass; "Colonial Quality, Samstag, New York, made in England"; $12.00.
9. USA; steel, rolled rim; $3.00.
10. England; brass, rolled rim, size 2; $7.00.
11. England; alloy; made for the American market; size 4; $7.00.

Row three:
1. Japan; celluloid, expandable, open top; c. 1975; $12.00.
2. Asia; bone, hand carved, top joined separately; c. 1850; $60.00.
3. Mexico; abalone over silver; octagonal, straight sides; c. 1980; $25.00.
4. Russia; figural painting on wood, black background; c. 1980; $7.50.
5. USA; gilded steel; wide band with hexagon design c. 1990; $7.50.
6. Russia; glazed pottery; stylized buildings, snow, flowers; 1" x 2"; $10.00.
7. Ireland; Belleck china; raised shamrock designs; 1970; ¾" x 1"; $35.00.
8. China; enamel inside and out, gilded top; decorative flowers and leaves; 1975; $8.00.
9. Asia; ivory, one piece, hand carved, delicate; c. 1850; $60.00.
10. China; .800 silver; expandable band; two seated women in historical dress working embroidery; $65.00.

Montgomery Ward & Co., Fall & Winter Catalogue No. 56, 1894 – 95.

Decorative thimble holders became very popular during the Victorian period. The finer thimbles of gold, silver, or mother-of-pearl came in boxes fitted for the shape of the thimble. The holders were traditional shapes but the most popular are the figural ones. The materials used were many. The practical use was the protection of the thimble and to make it easier to find the thimble when in its container.

England; white bisque shoe, decorative flowers; 10k thimble; c. 1890; $90.00.

1927 Edition of the Sears, Roebuck Catalogue, 1970.

Top row:
1. England; leather holder lined with paper and velvet; "Ladies Companion" in gold letters; thimble hallmark "Sterling, Birmingham, 1909"; 2" x 1" x ⅞"; $95.00.
2. USA; jewelers silk and velvet lined box; 14k Simons Bros. Co. Philadelphia; $110.00.
3. England; plush-covered hat box; brass latch; printed under the lid "Warranted solid silver, bottom Rd 16987; unmarked silver thimble; straight pins around the lining; $120.00.
4. England; trunk, brass trim, velvet cover and lining; brass latch; sterling thimble; "N.P." $145.00.

Row two:
1. England; book, decorative brass latch; Iles, Birmingham," silver cased thimble, Rd 16966; $65.00.
2. USA; Tiffany and Co., 5th Ave. & 27th St., New York, Paris, and London; gold lettering; 14k thimble; T & Co.; size 10; $250.00.
3. USA; Marshall Field's, Chicago; Waite Thresher Co., Providence, RI; "Martha"; c. 1920; size 5; $65.00.
4. USA; jeweler's thimble box, "Wm. Kindrick's Sons, Louisville, KY" houses Palais Royal Thimble (see single item photo, page 71).

Row three:
1. England; leather covered trunk, worn, brass latch, sterling thimble; decorative wheat band; c. 1875; $125.00.
2. USA; aluminum, bright-cut design, egg-shaped holder and aluminum thimble; $50.00.
3. USA; Mermod, Jacard & King, Jewelry Co., St. Louis, Est. 1829 Jacard's; sterling and 14k thimble; $100.00.
4. England; leather holder with silk lining; 10k; Ketcham McDougall, New York; size 8; $110.00.

Top row:

1, 3. Germany; Black Forest carvings; thimble holder and pincushion; perched bird; $90.00 – 120.00 each.

2. USA; cast-iron terrier, nickel finish; thimble holder "hat"; c. 1890; 3" x 2¼"; $75.00.

4. England; Barton Silver Co. "gnome" cast-iron thimble holder, cotton and silk thread on platform; sterling thimble, Simons Co.; 2" x 3"; $100.00.

Row two:

1. Germany; celluloid thimble holder; girl dressed in traditional Dutch costume and wooden shoes; sterling thimble; $90.00.

2. Germany; seated, china Cupid, painted face; sterling thimble four Cupids with garlands on the band; Webster Co., North Attleboro, MA; $235.00.

Row three:

1, 5. USA; crocheted wishbone thimble holders; sterling thimbles; 3¼" x 3"; $45.00 each.
   1. Wire rather than the traditional wishbone.

2, 3. Germany; Black Forest, hand-carved bears, glass eyes; $75.00 – 110.00 each.

4. Scotland; Mauchline transfer ware, Canterbury Cathedral; sterling thimble; 1¾" x 1¼"; $100.00.

Row four:

1. Asia; hand-carved vegetable ivory acorn, thimble made of the same piece of vegetable ivory inside; c. 1875; 2" x 1¼"; $135.00.

2. USA; painted metal bucket with handle, brass thimble; ¾" x ⅝"; $45.00.

3. USA; wood, telescope release; slight damage; 1¼"; $25.00.

4. Germany; molded metal; hinged terrier head, glass eyes, damaged sterling thimble in the jaw well; 1890; 2"; $150.00.

5. USA; carved stone, painted, metallic top; wood thimble post inside; c. 1980; $25.00.

6. England; turned-wood egg; c. 1880; $40.00.

Top row:

1. Japan; cloth shoe holder and pincushion; English brass thimble; c. 1920; $25.00.
2. Germany, Nurnberg; serving woman holding up the thimble in a bowl; velvet pincushion down the back of the skirt; c. 1850; $200.00.
3. Norway; lidded holder stand, sterling; stylized sea serpent, water bird designs; .830 silver thimble, green stone cap; c. 1875; $150.00.
4. France; brass cart, mother-of-pearl holder, brass trim, wheels roll, bronze dog dressed as man pulling cart; brass thimble; good condition; c. 1850; 2½" x 1½"; $225.00.

Row two:

1. Mexico; clear green onyx basket, crimped brass trim; unmarked gold thimble; 2" x 2½"; $95.00.
2. Mexico; trunk, sterling .930; velvet lining with raised feather designs, latch; unmarked sterling thimble, USA; c. 1950; 2" x 1"; $85.00.
3. Austria; gilded donkey and sleigh, mother-of-pearl, gilded trim dish; unmarked sterling thimble USA, note: "Miss Cassie Randolph gave me thimble in 1875 when I left school. I used it until 1915 and gave it to Sue."; monogram P.L.G; c. 1870; $225.00. (Thimble shown on page 72.)
4. Germany; leather slipper; velvet lining, leather sole, pin keep in arch of slipper, 10 straight pins; sterling thimble; 2¼" x ¾"; c. 1880; $100.00.

Row three:

1. Germany; hand-carved wooden lady's shoe, silk ribbon, and rose; brass thimble; 2½" x 1"; c. 1880; $50.00.
2. USA; Unger Bros., Newark, New Jersey; fine silver holder; Simons Bros. Co., sterling thimble band decorated with berries and vines; monogram "G"; size 9; $100.00.
3. USA; Webster Co; sterling walnut, Georgian style design, soft finish; 1½" x ¾"; $125.00.
4. England; plush bellows, brass trim; label "Le Soufflet Rd #138883, silver cased thimble"; $100.00.

Row four:

1. USA; Webster Co.; original box; sterling silver thimbles, .925 – 1000 fine; one dozen, size 9, thimbles made for "Domestic Sewing Machine," printed on the thimbles; never been used; $250.00.
2. England; metal stand, holder, bisque doll; sterling thimble with seaside scene on band; $98.00.

The Fleet Is In

Five sailing vessels are in harbor and one should be in dry dock. The six boats have mother-of-pearl sails, mollack hulls, brass riggings, including a loop to hold a thimble, and five have a pennant flying at the top of the mast. These boats were sea coast resort souvenirs, along with other shell items. They were popular at World's Fair Expositions, the last quarter of the nineteenth century and early twentieth century. The filigree brass boat is a stand-out in design and detail.

My son, Dan, has been my resource in trying to give each boat an identity. His comment was "A lot of artistic license is in these boats and creativity is required in giving them rigging identity."
Enjoy our effort.

Clockwise, beginning at 12:00:
1. Germany; two masted brig generic term square rigger; forward small sail souvenir, hand-painted flowers on second small sail; the nineteen rung ladder of pot metal could be representative of ratline, one of the small transverse ropes attached to the shrouds of a ship to form the steps of a rope ladder; six sails, sterling thimble, 4" x 6¾"; $120.00.
2. Fore-and-aft sails, gaff rig, hand painting on main sail "NE Cascades Building," "World's Fair St. Louis, MO 1904"; brass thimble; 4" x 5"; $135.00.
3. Germany; a tender, single square sail; small bisque figure of a young boy in a sailor's uniform of the nineteenth century; hand painting reads "A Present from Morecambe made in Germany" and flowers; anchor and chain at the bow; c. 1875; 4" x 4"; $125.00.
4. Asia; Dhow has latten rig brass filigree, not quite as detailed; cork post for the brass thimble, amethyst stone cap near the tiller; 6" x 2"; collection item; $200.00.
5. Lost hull; anchor and chain, lion's head prow; English brass thimble; c. 1890; $38.00.
6. Tender; single sail, oar; hand painted "World's Fair St. Louis, MO 1904"; brass thimble; $95.00.
7. Tender; hand-painted flowers and "From Atlantic City"; post for brass thimble; oar; $100.00.

Top row:
Sailing into the sunset, thimble holder; mother-of-pearl sails, jib reads "think of me," mainsail has painting
of boat sailing at sunset; brass thimble and base; 3½" x 4½"; $85.00.

Row 2:
1. France; wood carved thimble holder and needle holder; needles in handle, thimble in acorn; c. 1875; 4";
$105.00.
2. England; thimble holder, metal shoe covered with velvet, embroidered flower; sterling thimble; c. 1890; 2";
$75.00.

Row 3:
Three generations of a family's thimbles: Galbraith, Slaygle-Bell, and Nehring.
1. USA; Simons, 10k; monogram "Nannie"; twelve panel, six decorative designs and six plain; size 8; $110.00.
2. Ketcham & McDougall; 14k; ornate band design, monogram "B"; size 9; $120.00.
3. Unknown; 10k gold; top has been cut away, probably because it is easy to punch holes in gold with hard
use; monogram "R.T.B. 9.12.23"; size 9; $20.00.

Row four:
1. Simons; sterling, paneled band, has holes; size 6; $15.00.
2. Simons; sterling, wide paneled band, holes in side, size 9; $18.00.
3. Simons; "Priscilla," Pat. May 3/98; a plain and beaded band; holes in the side; size 11; $20.00.
4. Stern Bros.; sterling, floral band; bent and holes in edge of top; size 7; $12.00.

Row five:
1. England; domed brass thimble, large size; note in the thimble "Found in Civil War battleground at Fairfax
Station, Virginia"; the top is applied separately, rather than a solid mold; $50.00.

Thread:
Holders, Winders, Spools & Stands

During the eighteenth century England was manufacturing white sewing thread, also known as ounce thread. Scotland soon became the center for the major producers of thread. Storage of homespun was important because it tangled and soiled easily. Early sewing thread was sold by the pound or the skein.

Thread was wound on spindles that were then housed in small cotton barrels made of wood; bone, horn, or ivory. These thread barrels were often found in fitted sewing boxes of the early nineteenth century. Small holes drilled in the side of the barrels allowed the thread to be drawn out in lengths needed for a sewing project. By the 1840s needlework boxes were outfitted with reels (called spools in Ireland and USA, bobbins in Northern England) that had two discs for a top and base to hold the shank, one disc screwed on. The top was often decorative. Small thread winders were also tools in fitted boxes and used for silk thread. Reels were made to house commercially made thread. Because silk thread was fragile it was often wrapped on pieces of folded paper, wood, bone, ivory, or mother-of-pearl to prevent fraying. Chinese mother-of-pearl card game counters were often used as winders. Although they were rarely notched, they were inexpensive with attractive etched designs. Winders were also used for fine embroidery and cotton thread that came in skeins. Sterling winders have been popular and produced in the USA.

Reel table stands were not only useful but also decorative and they came in different heights and some had storage drawers. They were made of various woods, brass, iron, and steel. Victorian reel stands could have complex designs with the look of a piece of sculpture. Germany was the leading manufacturer of many novelty thread holders. W. and A. Smith manufacturers of Mauchline, tartan, and Tunbridge ware produced a variety of thread boxes and holders for 100 years. They were attractive, well made, and practical. Individuals made reel stands that were wall pieces and they ranged from a fine piece to primitive and each was functional.

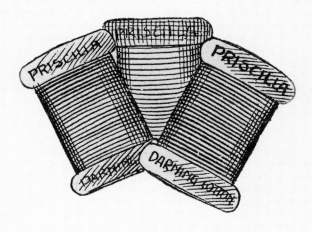

1897 Sears Roebuck Catalogue, 1968.

Top row:

1. USA, Canterbury, NH; thread reel or spool, wood; holds a large amount of thread; $50.00.
2, 4. Germany, Black Forest; wood carved bears seated; glass eyes; #2 has painted white teeth, hugging large spool; #4 on a stand, thread on a spindle and a container filled with a pincushion on bear's back; c. 1880; 3"; $95.00 – 110.00 each.
3. USA; commercial thread spool, wood; stamped "Kingston Baseball thread, 4 oz."; $7.00.

Row two:

1. USA; sterling thread holder; repoussé design; c. 1900; $125.00.
2. England; mother-of-pearl reel filled with silk thread; c. 1875; $60.00.
3. USA; La Piere, sterling holder; c. 1¼"; 1900; $95.00.

Row three:

1. England; ivory, carving dyed red; c. 1870; $90.00.
2. USA; hand-crocheted thimble basket; spool of cotton thread; c. 1930; $10.00.
3. USA; sterling thread bobbin holder; bobbin cover paper; c. 1915; $65.00.

Top row:

1. Ireland; bog oak thread, yarn, string holder; beehive shape; c. 1870; $65.00.
2. England; wood column for thread, three spools, three bone eyelets to dispense thread; c. 1875; $90.00.
3. England; closed wood container; houses eight spools of thread, each dispensed through bone eyelets. c. 1900; $85.00.
4. Japan; wood box, dispenser for yarn; black lacquer, gold painted scene on top; ivory eyelet; c. 1875; $75.00.

Row two:

1. USA; Tiffany & Co., #3153; sterling floral repoussé; c. 1900; $300.00.
2. Ireland; Bog oak barrel on low stand; thread and/or yarn holder; spout is the dispenser; c. 1875; $100.00.
3. USA; sterling thread holder with cutter; surface design waves; monogram "S.J."; c. 1920; $110.00.

Row three:

1. USA; sterling holder with cutter; decorative rims; monogram "G.S.H."; 1¼"; $125.00.
2. Unknown; ivory six-pointed star; hand-painted floral designs; 1½"; $30.00.
3. Unknown; ivory thread holder disc; four partial circles for winding thread, red thread; 2"; $55.00.
4. England; thread waxer, gilded metal cover at both ends of work reel; floral designs; ¾"; $70.00.
5. Asia; hand-carved vegetable ivory holder; screw top; c. 1860; $55.00.

Top row:
1. USA; beeswax for thread, dome mold; $7.00.
2. USA; winder, decorative cardboard; handmade; c. 1900; $8.00.
3. USA; beeswax mold around Frozen Charlotte above the elbow; ribbon hanger; c. 1915; collection item; $50.00.

Row two:
1. USA; Frozen Charlotte molded in beeswax up to the elbow; the beeswax used to pull thread through, made stitching smoother; c. 1915; collection item; $50.00.
2. Asia; pie-shaped beeswax mold; embedded silk ribbon; c. 1900; $9.00.
3. USA; fine yarn winder, large four prongs, celluloid; c. 1920; $55.00.

Row three:
1. England; six-prong wood winder, three different threads wrapped; c. 1900; $35.00.
2. England; ivory rectangle, concave sides, pointed corners; c. 1890; $20.00.
3. USA; beeswax mold with honey bee relief; a disc; c. 1920; $15.00.

Row four:
1. USA; wood, square, decorative carved edge; c. 1890; $35.00.
2. Scotland, Mauchline; six-pointed wooden star; etching transfer "A View of Brighton Pavilion"; c. 1890; $80.00.
3. – 4. USA; simple winders used for small amounts of silk thread; #3 hand-cut celluloid; #4 bone; $2.00 – 8.00 each.

Top row:

1 – 4. England; mother-of-pearl thread winders.

    1. Disc, scalloped edge; $48.00.

    2, 3. Six prongs, fluted edges; $15.00 each.

    4. Four prongs, rounded ends; $32.00.

    5. Ivory; complex design and edge; c. 1860; $65.00.

Row two:

1. USA; glass winder two very thin layers of glass molded and cut with four prongs; c. 1920; $45.00.

2. USA; bead edge, sterling rectangle, four curled prongs; c. 1920; $95.00.

3. USA; sterling, floral designs on the four prongs; c. 1900; $60.00.

4. USA; bone winder; concave; $18.00.

Row three:

1, 2. Two sets of commercial abalone tools; punch, tatting shuttle, thread winder; original display card, "Genuine Abalone Shell"; c. 1915; $60.00 each set.

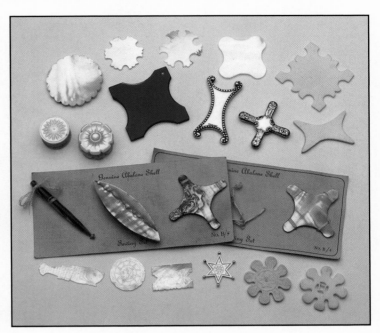

Row four:

1 – 3. China; mother-of-pearl, fish, disc, rectangle; c. 1860; $18.00 each.

4. Brass; six prong; decorative designs; knobbed points; $35.00.

5. China; ivory; intricate designs on face on winder; c. 1875; $30.00.

6. China; ivory; carved opening in center; c. 1880; $28.00.

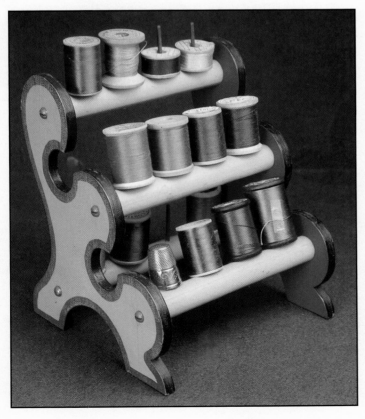

England; Art Deco wood silk thread stand, painted, three levels, 14 spools of silk thread, sterling thimble; classic color choices; c. 1920; $145.00.

1. England; turned stand and lifts, six thread spindles, silk covered pincushion; silk thread; c. 1900; 4"; $48.00.
2. USA; desk thread stand; tambour sliding doors; pincushion attached to second shelf, storage drawer at base; deep; Patent May 18, 1800; owner Flora T. Ham; 8½"w. x 10"h. x 4½"; $250.00.
3. USA; wood stand, steel spikes with top knot holds spools on stand, they lift up for changing; silk thread; decorative wood tear-drop at the top; c. 1880; 6½"; $110.00.

1. USA; wood, handcrafted; eight wood spikes holding spools; storage drawer; c. 1915; 6"; $35.00.
2. USA, New Hampshire; wood wall thread stand, handmade; storage drawer; c. 1870; 9"; $70.00.
3. USA; two tier, turned wood, twelve-spool thread stand; velvet cushion; c. 1900; $40.00.

1. USA, Massachusetts; painted, wood, eight-spool thread wall stand with large storage drawer; c. 1860; $78.00.
2. USA; female server holding thread on trays; commercially produced, souvenir; c. 1930; $48.00.

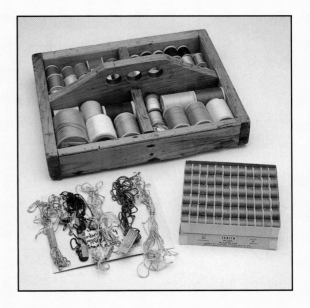

Left to right:
1. USA; thread carrier; may have been a tool box before it was refinished; forty spools of silk thread; c. 1900; $75.00.
2. USA; Sylvan Silk Embroidery rope; displayed on sale card; c. 1920; $5.00 each.
3. USA, Mt. Holly, N.C.; "Zenith American & Efred Thread Mills"; ice blue cotton, size oo, cardboard discs cover bobbin; $15.00 box.

USA; shaker hand-woven yarn holder for continuous needlework; the yarn is dispensed through lined hole in top; beautiful design and workmanship; collection item; $440.00.

Top row:
1. Corticelli spools of silk thread, six large spools of red thread, four medium red spools, four small white spools, original box; $18.00.

Row 2:
1. England; turned wood, three winder units; c. 1900; $35.00.
2. China; eight arms, mother-of-pearl silk thread winder; $40.00.
3. USA; handmade, wood, gold letters "WBS"; ¾" x 1½"; $12.00.
4. Scotland; Turnbridge ware, waxen, 1½"; c. 1880; $40.00.

Row 3 and 4:
China; wood, stained lacquered finish.
1. Scalloped flower, 2½"; $110.00.
2. Square, curved corners; 3½"; $115.00.
3. Curved column, 2" x 6"; $120.00.

Advertising and trade cars were used by manufacturers to attract both women and men to their products. The multicolored ones were particular favorites of women. The variety in these cards represent the creative ability of the artisans; there's humorous, caring, and sedate; using animals and individuals of all ages, as well as patriotic and political themes.

USA; J & P Coasts Best Six Cord; 1890; $5.00 – 25.00.
Top row:
1. "We never fade."
2. Face in a flower; 1887.
3. "Black, white, and colors"; "See Saw in the Hedge, which is the way to the London Bridge."
4. Best six cord thread

Row two:
1. J & P Coats Best Six Cord; trio reading the paper
2. Cats tormenting dog restrained by Clark's thread
3. Clark's Mill End; big wheel bike wins with Clark's
4. Bad man tripped up by Clark's

Row three:
1. Clark's Mill End; beautiful girl carrying wheat
2. Keeping him tied up by Clark's
3. Merrick Thread Co; "Won't come off Grandpa'
4. Best 6 cord
5. "Liberty enlightens"

Row four:
1. Merrick Thread Co.; free as a butterfly, strong as the wind
2. Willimantic thread; "Jumbo must go, drawn by Willimantic"
3. "I will put a girdle of (Willimantic Thread) round about the World in forty minutes."

1897 Sears Roebuck Catalogue, 1968.

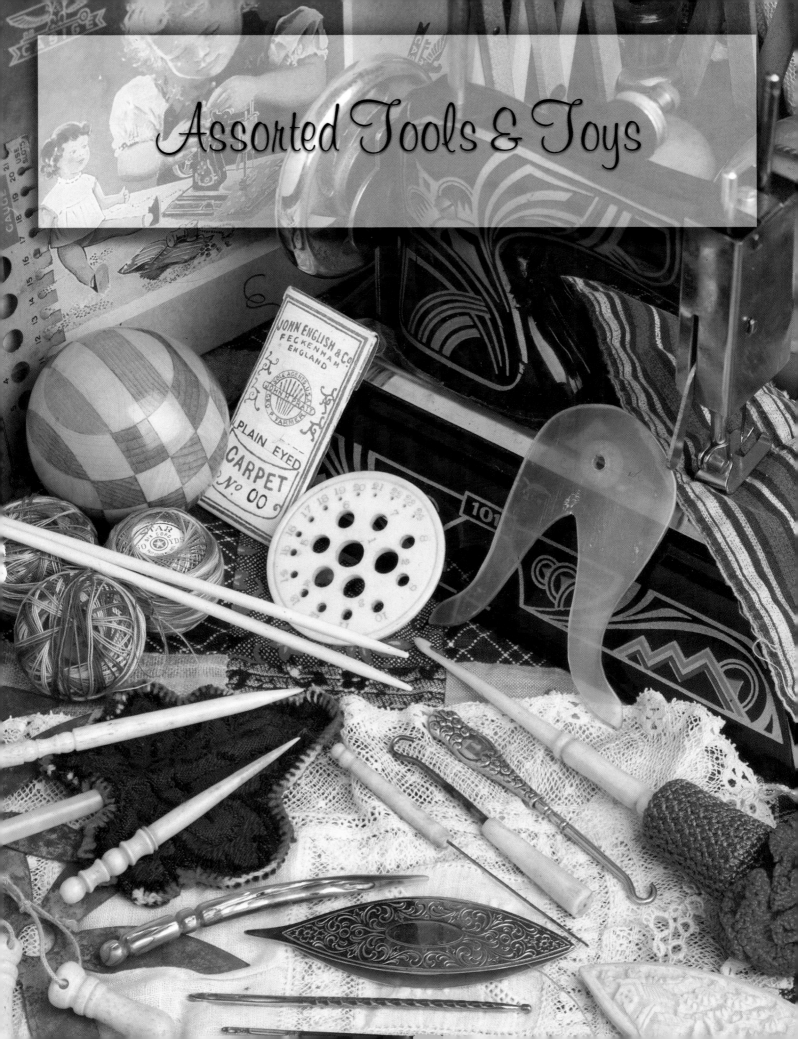

Assorted Tools & Toys

The needlework tools in this chapter represent not only tools of necessity but also beyond the ordinary. Knitting came to England by way of Italy and through Scotland. Knitting sheaths go back to the 1600s, but finding any much before 1900 is unlikely. Early ones were handmade and of poor quality.

The knitting needle guards are much smaller and used for a different purpose. There were simple turned pairs and delightful figural pairs made of ivory, wood, silver, and other materials. They protected the points and kept stitches from coming off the ends. The guards had small holes near the rim to thread on the braid, and elastic, or chain for holding them together. The joining material is often missing but easily replaced. Be sure that the guards are a matching pair.

Crochet is a French word meaning "little hook." Crochet is basically a chain stitch, added in order to create more complex patterns. Gay Ann Rogers writes that it became popular in the Atlantic states in the second quarter of the nineteenth century, in Europe as early as the Renaissance. The hooks were available as a single, complete item or as a kit with a handle and several different sizes of interchangeable hooks.

The lucet was used for making chains and braid. The chains were used sometimes for clothing fasteners. The stiletto or punch pierced the fabric or embroidery to make a hole without damaging the fibers. The lucet is a rare item, harder to find, thus more expensive. The stilletto was often one tool of a sewing kit.

See pillow and lacemaking bobbins on page 102, lacemaking pillow on page 103, photograph of lacemakers on page 103.

Tatting was made with a skillful knotting techniques giving it a lace quality. When different designs were wanted, needle and thread, as well as small shuttles, were used to sew it together until the knotting shuttle was designed to work with the original shuttle. The knotting shuttle is larger and has rounded ends. The interest in tatting declined after WWI. Early shuttles were made of precious metals, later more affordable materials such as wood, bone, steel, and celluloid were used.

Illustration from *The Mary Frances Sewing Book* Jane Eayre Fryer.

1. Aluminum hexagon quilt pattern, for pieced quilts; c. 1975; $5.00.
2. New England; tin stencil for quilting designs; c. 1900; $40.00.
3. USA; set of flat lead pencils, silver-plate pencil holder decorative flowers; original box; Eberhard Faber Mfr.; $28.00.
4. USA; Pennsylvania; hand cut quilting stencil; paper; c. 1900; $35.00.
5. USA; New England; handmade tin stencil; the descending stars get larger; c. 1900; $40.00 each.

Top row:
1. Belgium; scattered handmade lace butterflies; various sizes; gift to author by maker; 1985; $20.00 each.
2. USA; bride's handmade lace handkerchief; rows of lace and one row of netting; embroidered 6/2/72; $25.00.

Row two:
1. England; blouse neck decoration; c. 1915; $18.00.
2 – 4. England; lacemaking needles.
    2. Wood, hand carved; $20.00.
    3. Wood, hand carved; $15.00.
    4. Ivory; $25.00.

Row three:
1. Antimaccar braid; Pat. 1000, warranted twelve yards, no. 2; c. 1910; $9.00.
2. Beautiful, handmade lace collar; netting on the inside edge to attach to garment; 1900; $25.00.

USA; stencil and calico glass buttons; set up as a sales display; variety of sizes; c. 1900; $2.00 – 3.00 each.

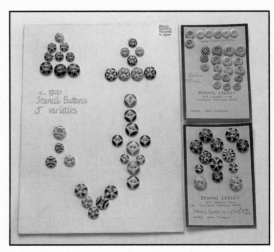

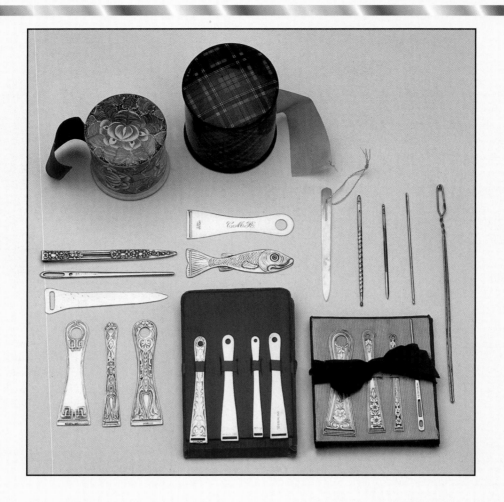

Top row:
1. England; beautiful hand-painted wood ribbon dispenser, opening in the side; c. 1875; $65.00.
2. Scotland; tartan ware ribbon dispenser, opening on the side; c. 1880; $125.00.

Row two:
1 – 5. Five different styles of sterling bodkins used to thread ribbon, braid, yarn, or string through hems, waist bands, storage bags, and cut work.
    1. France; slide to fit size of ribbon being used; $95.00.
    2. Bodkin needle; $30.00.
    3. Handcrafted, hammered design; $45.00.
    4. CB&H; monogram "C.M.R"; $58.00.
    5. England; fish; two slits for ribbon tail and mouth; $150.00.
6. USA; mother-of-pearl; $12.00.
7. USA; brass bodkin needle; $6.00.
8. USA; bodkin needle; brass and enamel; $7.00.
9. USA; steel bodkin needle $6.00.
10. USA; brass with safety pin pull; 7"; $12.00.

Row three:
1. Sterling, Greek key design; c. 1920; 4"; $45.00.
2, 3. Two of a matching set; sterling; Art Nouveau design; c. 1900; $55.00 each.
4 – 5. Two sets of four; partial match; sterling.
    4. Red case set, second and third matching F & B; fourth Simons; $110.00 set.
    5. Light case set, first Art Nouveau design; second and third matching holly hock design; fourth F & B needle bodkin; $120.00 set.

Top row:
Tatting edging winding around display, variety tatting shuttles.
1. Four bone shuttles; fourth has work in progress; c. 1930; $20.00 –
40.00 each.

Row two:
1. USA; steel, etched designs; $15.00.
2. USA; Bakelite; $6.00.
3. USA; wood tatting shuttle; $10.00.
4. Tatting kit; basket by Native Americans; stores shuttle, thread, and
scissors; c. 1930; $28.00.

Row three:
1. Ivory; $40.00.
2. Mother-of-pearl; $28.00.
3. USA; advertisement; Lydia Pinkham, vegetable compound; celluloid;
c. 1920; $95.00.
4. Sterling; beautiful, cut work design; $90.00.
5. China; ivory; detailed carving; $110.00.
6. Two spools tatting thread; $2.00.
7. USA; tatting medallion; decorative household item, c. 1920 – 30; $10.00.

USA, Kansas; sign on porch, "Mrs. E.N.
Brown Dressmaker"; $25.00.
Wooden box of cut steel, decorative buttons;
c. 1920; $25.00 for all.

USA; beautiful, handwork embroidery on linen apron; satin ribbon
ties; "A Stitch in Time Saves Nine"; girl sewing button on for young
boy; spool thread and needle, scissors, thimble; top right: reverse glass
painting of lady in parlor embroidering, framed; c. 1900; center: red
wool, hand embroidery, mantle display item; c. 1890; top left: lace
edging on linen handkerchief; four units of red thread embroidery;
$50.00 apron; $75.00 painting; $30.00 handkerchief; $7.00.

Although button hooks are not sewing tools, they were needed as a result of sewing and fashion styles. It is common to see them in vanity sets, sewing boxes, and shaving kits. They were used to button shoes and clothing. The Victorians enjoyed having the practical ones as well as those made of metal, mother-of-pearl, and ivory. Manufacturers and businesses used them for advertising. They are a delight to collect because of the many unusual designs and sizes. Generally they are affordable, be patient and selective.

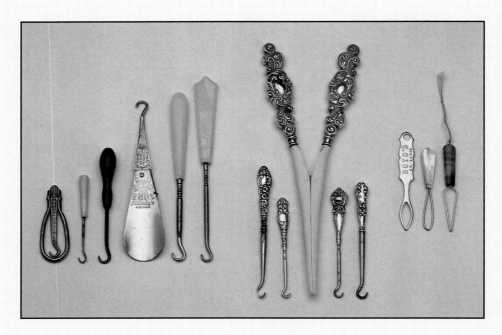

Buttonhooks:
1. Steel, folding, when open has a handle; TM Deposé, design on hook handle; c. 1890; $10.00.
2. Bone handle, steel hook; c. 1910; $3.00.
3. Black wood handle, steel hook; c. 1900; $3.00.
4. Steel shoe horn and hook, "Milady's Shoehorn," "patent pending"; etched designs; c. 1875; $25.00.
5, 6. Bakelite handles, steel hooks; #6 was part of a dresser set; c. 1930; $4.00 – 8.00 each.
7, 8, 10, 11. Sterling handles, steel hooks; c. 1880 – 1910; $20.00 – 45.00 each.
9. Glove stretcher, sterling handles, ivory stretchers; seen occasionally, rarely used; c. 1880; $55.00.
12 – 14. These three hooks were used to protect fragile fabrics, usually short.
    12. USA; steel; advertising "Boyd's, St. Louis" ; scalloped handle; $10.00.
    13. Mother-of-pearl handle, brass hook, note round end; $12.00.
    14. Agate handle, tassel; brass hook; $17.00.

Top row:

The Punch was used whenever a round hole was needed for shoes, belts, clothing, and other farm and home items. When cut work embroidery was completed a punch was used to break away fibers to show off embroidery work.

1 – 4. Asia; c. 1850; $10.00 –18.00 each.
    1. Abalone
    2. Ivory
    3. Mother-of-pearl
    4. Hand-carved leg and shoe

Row two:

1, 4. Ivory; $8.00 each.

2, 3. Bone; $4.00 each.

5, 6. Sterling, polished steel; screw gage to adjust size hole needed; $38.00 each.

7. Tracing wheel, sterling and steel; $42.00.

8. Tracing wheel, wood, hand-carved bean pod; recessed steel wheel; $18.00.

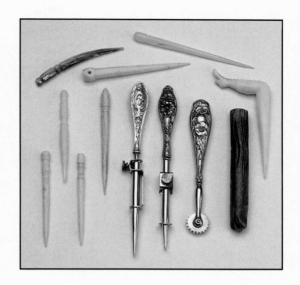

Top row:

1. England; crochet hook holder, painted wood, c. 1875; $35.00.

2. Germany; holder fitted with one screw handle and three hooks, different sizes; c. 1900; $45.00.

3. Wood holder, four steel hooks, different sizes; $20.00.

4. Wood holder, one screw handle, four ivory hooks; c. 1900; $42.00.

5. Crocheted baby bootie, summer wear; c. 1930; $5.00.

Row two:

1. Lady's linen handkerchief; hand crocheted edging; c. 1920; $7.00.

2. USA; hand crochet edging for household linens; eight yards; c. 1940; $16.00.

Display of assorted crochet hooks:

3, 4. Bone, #4 double hook; $3.00 – 4.00 each.

5. USA, Florida; ivory, souvenir; carved orange at top, hand painted; $12.00.

6. China; hand-carved, dog sitting on top of column; c. 1900; $55.00.

7. Grouping, five bone hooks; $3.00 – 6.00 each.

8. Enamel, floral design handle, bone hook; c. 1915; $12.00.

9. Bakelite handle, steel hook; $5.00.

10. Brass hook with ring; $5.00.

11. Turned bone handle, steel hook; $8.00.

12. Steel, twist handle; hook at one end, small darning egg the other; c. 1900; $14.00.

13. Bone, double hook; $10.00.

14. Pair of window shade pulls, hand crocheted; c. 1920; $10.00.

15. Clarks' ONT spool of crochet thread; c. 1940; $2.00.

1923 Sears, Roebuck Catalogue, 1973.

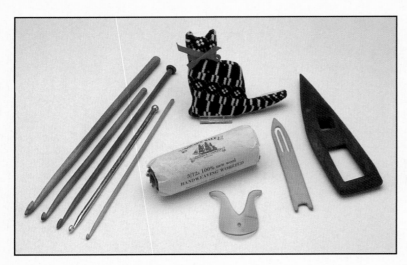

Top row:
Small stuffed cat, scrap of hand woven 1875 coverlet from Pennsylvania; c. 1976; $28.00.

Row two:
1. Five individual knitting needles, four wood, one aluminum; $6.00 each pair.
2. "Square Sale," "Frederick J. Fawsett, Boston Mass." "100% wool, hand weaving worsted"; $3.00.
3. Netting needle used in lacemaking; wood; $15.00.
4. Fisherman's wood netting needle, hand crafted; c. 1900; $24.00.

Row three:
1. Bakelite lucet for braid making; $20.00.

1. Two pair wood knitting needles, one single; $10.00.
2. Pair knitting needle guards, ivory; 7" steel needles; c. 1890; $58.00.
3. Two pair; one bone, one ivory, knitting needle guards; c. 1890; 1½"; $24.00 pair.
4. USA, New England; handmade walnut Niddy Noddy for winding skeins of yarn; c. 1900; $48.00.
5. Handmade crochet guard, celluloid holder inside; c. 1920; $5.00.
6. Trade card and advertisement, Eureka knitting silk thread; parlor scene with mother knitting; c. 1910; $8.00.
7. Rinso knitting pin gauge, "Use Rinso for every kind of washing"; sizes 1 through 24; $10.00.
8. Germany; assorted knitting needle sizes; container tin, delightful colors, art, and lettering; No. 117; c. 1915; $40.00.
9. The Run Mender, "Takes runs out of silk hose and lingerie completely"; very small latch hook and paper with instructions; c. 1930; $5.00.
10. Handmade knitting needle guard; $2.00.
11. Dritz Needle Home Repair Kit No. 616; for mattress, carpet, sails or tents, upholstery, packing, and gloves; paper with information and needles; 1940; $4.00.

Top row:

1 – 3. Fabric labels

    1. "Premiere Qualite"; 45" long, 144" wide; c. 1867; $18.00.

    2. "Uxbridge Mills Fine Shirting." Manfr. By J.F. Whitin, Whitinsville, Mass; c. 1867; $18.00.

    3. "Bruner's Balmoral Skirt"; Philadelphia, Warranted Fast Colors," size 144" x 45"; c. 1867; $20.00.

Row two:

1. USA, Toledo, Ohio; T.B. Terry & Co.; Patented April 21, 1885; Lansing Cooperative Asso, North Lansing, Michigan; knives and scissors; $8.00.

Row three:

1. "W.T. Moore & Co, dress goods and silks"; Chicago; $5.00.

2. Advertising card; "Compliments of Mrs. F.M. Huff, Milliner, Warren, In."; $7.00.

3. Portrait of lady, beautiful lace collar; advertising, Mandel Brothers, Chicago; fine European fabrics and outer garments; 1887 – 88; $4.00.

Row four:

1. Dressmaker or tailors' scissors; stamped "Est. 1847"; $35.00.

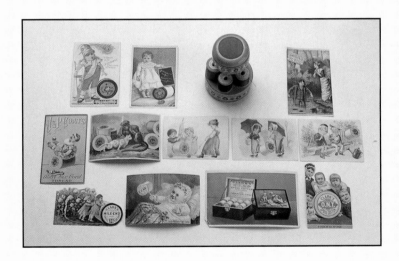

Trading cards to advertise thread products, children and animals two of the favorite subjects used.

Top row:

1, 2. Two Willimantic thread; $7.00 – 10.00 each.

3. USA; five spool thread stand with pincushion, J & P Coats thread; decorative geometrics; souvenir; c. 1920; $22.00.

4. Corticelli "silk spool and twist"; $5.00.

Row two:

Five J & P Coats advertising trade cards; $4.00 – 10.00 each.

Row three:

Four Clark's "Millend," "ONT"; third card shows Mauchline thread box, top with young girl and dog; c. 1875; $3.00 – 12.00 each.

Lacemaking bobbins are identified with the Midlands of England. Many were handcrafted and were stored carefully when not in use. The bobbins in the photo represent one collectors eye for the unusual. The painted designs, how they are personalized, and the sets of seven beads on each bobbin represents beauty in tools as well as the lace that was made by hand with these very tools.

Doll is made of composition, glass eyes with lids that open and close, arms jointed at arm holes, legs jointed at the hips; mohair wig; wearing a velvet dress with wide lace, lace jabo, lace trimmed velvet cap; seated in high back wooden chair with lacemaking pillow on stand in front of her; 5"; c. 1875; $225.00.

Bobbins; $25.00 – 65.00 each.
1. Ivory; series of carved rings painted red and black.
2. Wood stained; raised ribs, decorative pewter designs.
3. Ivory; angled, painted lines and indentations.
4. Wood; "Love" spelled with small indentations.
5. Bone; "Daniel," sets of three painted rings.
6. Ivory; lettering "Victoria" wraps around the bobbin; rings painted red.
7. Ivory; "Prince Albert" spelled with red painted indentations.
8. Ivory; "William Colby" in red, black, blue letters.
9. Wood; decorative pewter rings.
10. Ivory; wrapped with brass wire; red and black painted indentations.

France; Angoulême, southeast of Paris; lacemaking in progress; pins act as guides and are moved when pattern unit complete; the pillow is covered with oil cloth, underneath is covered with sacking, twenty-three wood bobbins; patterns are perforated, six stored in back of pillow; floral lace trim and monogram "MG" saved from a girl's bodice; green trim oil cloth; in use by family for 60 years; 10" x 10" x 4"; $225.00.

Belgium, Brussels; postcard of lacemakers working with their pillow and bobbins; Brussels lace is described as "various fine needlepoint or bobbin laces made with floral designs made originally in or near Brussels"; c. 1915; $5.00.

1. Holland; HM sterling; knitting needle guards with pair of 7" celluloid needles; decorative bright-cut waves cresting; expandable chain; c. 1875; 2½"; $100.00.
2. Northern Europe; knitting needle sheath, silver; beautiful repoussé, woman's head, pair of hearts, urn, large bouquet, cluster of fruit at the bottom; thought to be a gift to a loved one; back has a cover of sheet silver, two belt loops attached, sheath cylinder attached high on back; the women were accomplished knitters; the cold climate required many different clothing items, as well bed covers; a stationary needle at the hip, possibly a child on the other or herding sheep, the necessities could be completed; it was not uncommon to see woman at all these tasks at once. Collection item; NPA.

1. Germany; varnished wood box, "The Singer Manfg. Co." with trademark, on top "Naehmaschinen, Singer Die Besten"; seven holes for machine needles, 9, 11, 13, 14, 16, 18; c. 1900; 2½", $48.00.
2. Germany; two wash dress trimmings, machine embroidery, 3 yards, washing instructions label on back of package, recommends Ivory Soap; 2¼" x 7"; c. 1910; $15.00 each.
3. USA; Susan Bates Knit Check, Chester, Conn.; "Quality since 1873; stitch measure instructions, holes for knitting needle sizes, 000-16; crochet hook sizes B-N; US standard sizes; aluminum; 6"; c. 1960; $8.00.
4. USA; decorative table medallion, hand embroidered; embroidery worked on silk net, border metallic gold thread crochet; 5½" x 6½"; c. 1915; $18.00.

Clockwise:
1. USA, Utica, NY; Singer Sewhandy Model 20; nickel-plated sewing plate, gear driven; thread route numbered, spiral hand wheel, chain stitch; c. 1950; $120.00.
2. Germany; Casige, scroll and red floral designs; c. 1930; 7½" x 4¼" x 8"; $98.00.
3. Germany; Muller, model number 7c; sheet metal; bird and berries designs; $100.00.
4. Germany; Casige; red poppy designs front and back; "made in Germany, British Zone" stamped on sewing plate; c. 1950; $110.00.

Needlecraft Magazine, February 1938.

1. USA; Singer machine oil glass bottle; c. 1920; $15.00.
2. Germany; Casige number 1015; original box and instructions, key, screwdriver, table clamp; $250.00.
3. Germany; Casige; sheet metal; scroll and floral designs; c. 1930; $85.00.
4. Germany,; small floral design; 3" x 5"; c. 1930; $100.00.

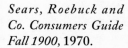

Sears, Roebuck and Co. Consumers Guide Fall 1900, 1970.

1. USA Singer "20" machine for girls, not a toy; originally boxed with machine, needles, thread, table clamp; nickel-plated sewing plate; 1927; $110.00.
2. Trading and advertising cards; Household Sewing Machine Co; "the Love" makes better buttonholes on any fabric, Wheeler and Wilcox; Singer; a hand out at the World Columbian Exhibit 1895 Chicago, Illinois, Liberal Arts Building; New Home Sewing Machine, Standard Sewing Machine; c. 1875 – 1925; $2.00 – 25.00.
3. Two tintypes; woman sewing at treadle machine and three women sewing; c. 1860; collection items; $125.00 each.

Top row:
1. USA; Frye wooden ware, known for round and oval boxes; Mill water powered since 1855; the Canterbury Shakers contracted Frye to produce their style boxes; lined and outfitted with thimble holder, pincushion, needle case, matching wood thimble, button box; collection item; $150.00.
2. Ornament in original box, "Sew Darn Cute," sewing mouse, pincushion, thread stand, stocking on a line; $35.00.
3. USA; pottery, "Thimbelina" by Tom Clark; kerchief on head, topped with a brass thimble, holding thread and sitting on a spool; c. 1988; $30.00.

Row two:
1. USA; "Sterling Silver" Christmas Pudding Charms; thimble one of eight charms; used by families in the U.S. during special holidays and festivals; 1950; $50.00.
2. Precious Moments, "Good Friends Share So Much"; two girls sewing on holiday stocking, background sewing machine, mice; $35.00.
3. USA; holiday ornament, mouse on spool of thread; c. 1980; $7.00.
4. USA; handmade felt clown with sequins, painted spool of thread; c. 1970; $10.00.

Row three:
1. USA; small bear sitting on a thimble, holiday ornament; c. 1980; $8.00.
2. USA; nickel silver needle case; c. 1940; $25.00.
3. Taiwan; reproduction sterling thimble holder; decorative single petal roses; c. 1980; $45.00.
4. Sterling silver "Birthday Cake Set," Webster Co.; blackened sterling; original box, display card; thimble one of eight; $60.00.
5. China; enamel over brass needle holder; reproduction; 1985; $35.00.
6. USA; three small hotel sewing kits; 1985 – 99; $2.00 – 5.00 each.

Row four:
1. USA; necklace, stork, scissors, and thimble charms, 10K gold; 1986; $65.00.

Underneath:
1. USA, New England; sampler made by C. Perkins, age 13; cross-stitch alphabet, floral vines; one edge worn, loss of some lettering; dated 1813; $70.00.
2. USA; patchwork doll quilt, c. 1950; $30.00.

Top row:
1. USA; wool felt mitten needle holder; handmade; c. 1920; $12.00.
2. USA; child's sewing kit, original box plaid paper outer cover; five compartments, pins, needles, needle threader, velvet pincushion, thimble, and thread; c. 1925; $25.00.
3. England; child's "Companion," travel sewing kit, six cut steel tools, leather cover; c. 1860; $75.00.
4. USA; framed lettering and sewing exercise, "Lord Be Thou My Helper"; silk thread; c. 1915; $10.00.
5. France; child's etui, leather; tools; c. 1860; $65.00.
6. USA; child's toy iron; copy of a sad iron; c. 1910; $20.00.

Row two:
1. USA; McCall doll dress pattern, also patterns for slip, panties, bonnet; directions on back; c. 1930; $9.00.
2. USA, New England; china head with homemade soft body and clothes; c. 1900; $45.00.
3. USA; card of 12 mother-of-pearl buttons; c. 1920; $5.00; doll nightie patterns; $10.00.
4. USA; little girls' sad irons; each on a stand; one shaped like a swan; c. 1900; $40.00 each.

Row three:
1. USA; girl's coin purse with 1915 penny; metal clasp; $20.00.
2. England; girl's coin purse, lizard skin, metal clasp; some wear; $15.00.
3. USA; felt fold-up; girl's sewing kit; appliqué stars, handmade; c. 1940; $5.00.
4. Metal embroidery hoop, cork spring ring, easy on, easy off, holds handwork tight; c. 1920; $7.00.
5. Ten thimbles, various sizes for girls; eight sterling, one aluminum, one steel; c. 1920 – 50; sterling; $20.00; aluminum, $5.00.
6. USA, Pennsylvania; handmade Amish hooked rug, doll house or playhouse; 4½"; $65.00.

Row four:
1. USA and England; four pair of gilt and polished steel miniature scissors; also used as charms; $18.00 each.
2. England; Victorian scene on brass, child's tablet with pencil; c. 1880; $20.00.
3. USA; round ends, steel school scissors; c. 1900; 4"; $10.00.
4. USA; practice sewing card, elephant; there were a number of different images in the sets that appealed to boys and girls of various ages; c. 1920 – 40; $5.00.

Scissors, Knives & Cutters
Tape Measures, Rulers & Gauges

Scissors, Knives & Cutters

Scissors have a long history that pre-dates the Roman Empire by 2000 years. They were a spring blade shear, not unlike sheep shears. Their use was widespread by craftsmen, farmers, and within households. During the Roman period the cross blade scissors with a center pivot were introduced.

Prior to 1830 scissors were handcrafted. These high quality tools continued to be handcrafted into the twentieth century. Although the Sheffield, England, steel mills produced very high quality steel that was imported by other countries to make cutlery, England did not produce cutlery items until the nineteenth century. Items with the "Sheffield" stamp have been identified as very high quality for 200 years.

Small scissors were often made of steel but larger scissors continued to be made of iron until 1860. During the Empire period, the French manufacturers were the early producers of unique scissor handles, introducing different materials such as mother-of-pearl. By the late nineteenth century scissors became statements of Victorian style with silver handles, ornate sheaths, and later with Art Nouveau and Art Deco designs in silver, gold, and gilt over silver.

Production of scissors continued to be expensive and the blades produced in 1870s did not hold a sharp edge. The hot drop-forged process did finally eliminate this problem. The quality and low prices of the German manufacturers of cutlery surpassed other countries and they had both the French and American markets. It is interesting to note there was iron and steel items produced in Solingen, Germany, beginning during the fourteenth century.

Gay Ann Rogers writes that the Butterick Co. in 1895 sold English made "stork" scissors for 50¢ and plain scissors for 25¢. The "stork" and other animal shaped handles were first popularized by John Rogers and Sons and Thomas Wilkinson and Sons of Seffield, England, during the mid-nineteenth century. The English detail work was of higher quality than either the American or German.

Buttonhole scissors were available by 1894. As a result of the Empire period the small, handy Chinese scissors found a market in Europe and the United States.

When cataloging these collection pieces, look for the manufacturer's mark near the pivot, and silver handles that are hallmarked or stamped "sterling." Sometimes you will need a jewelers' loupe to find the mark. Country of origin would be both countries when marked.

Sears, Roebuck and Co. Catalog No. 157 Fall and Winter 1928–29, 1928.

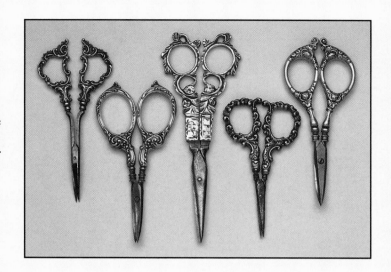

Left to right:
1, 2, 4, 5. USA; sterling embroidery scissors; decorative designs, short blades; c. 1900; $45.00 – 70.00 each.
3. Germany; .800 silver; unusually long handles for embroidery length blades; c. 1900; $65.00.

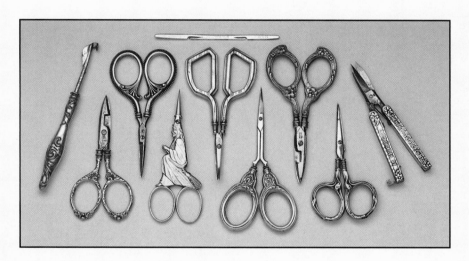

Top row:
1. USA, thread cutter, double, sterling; Pat. March 24, 1903; $25.00.

Row two:
1. USA; button thread cutter; W-C Co.; silver plate; Pat. Jan. 5, 1892, 5"; $20.00.
2. USA; Art Nouveau flowing leaves, beaded trim handles; sterling; $55.00.
3. USA & Germany; JM Benz Co.; sterling; Art Deco; c. 1920; $50.00.
4. USA & Germany; sterling buttonhole scissors; ornate lilies, daisies; $65.00.
5. USA; fold-up snips, sterling; advertising "compliments of the Home Ins. Co., NY"; floral design handles; $45.00.

Row three:
1. USA & Germany; Gorham sterling handles; German blades; buttonhole scissors; c. 1894; $75.00.
2. USA; Salem Witch, gilded, reproduction; $50.00.
3. USA; .800 silver handles, steel blades; c. 1920; $45.00.
4. USA; Art Deco design; embroidery; c. 1920; $55.00.

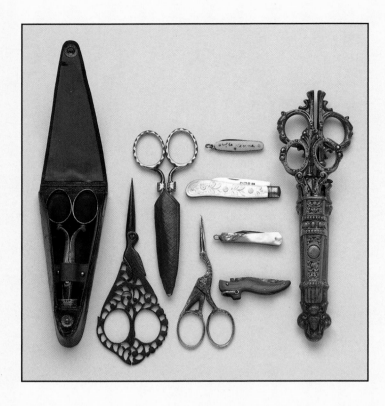

1. Germany; steel scissors and brass "DRGM" thimble set in leather box lined with silk & velvet; c. 1895; 4½"; $98.00.
2. England; iron stork scissors, unusual open work, winged handles; c. 1860; 5½"; $110.00.
3. England; cut steel scissors in red leather sheath; c. 1860; 4½"; $75.00.
4. USA; steel stork scissors; nickel polish rubbed off; c. 1914; 4"; $15.00.
5. England, lady's knife, ivory cover, single steel blade; c. 1870; 1½"; $20.00.
6. England, London; HM sterling knife, decorative mother-of-pearl; sterling blade; $95.00.
7. Asia; abalone lady's knife; one steel blade; c. 1900, 2"; $20.00.
8. USA; lady's shoe, knife, one blade, c. 1900; $15.00.
9. Germany; ornate pair of scissors in paired sheath; c. 1870; 7"; $100.00.

1. USA; sterling; L. S & B; plain; 5"; $50.00.
2. Spain; gilded stork scissors, souvenir of "Toledo"; enamel work on beak; c. 1985 reproduction; $25.00.
3. USA; "F & B"; sterling, double beading on handles; c. 1915; 4"; $40.00.

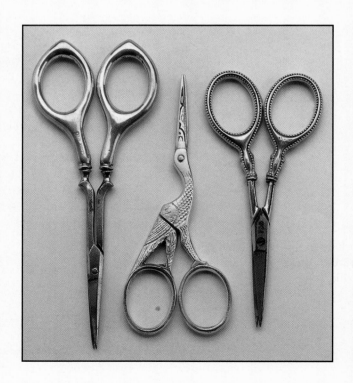

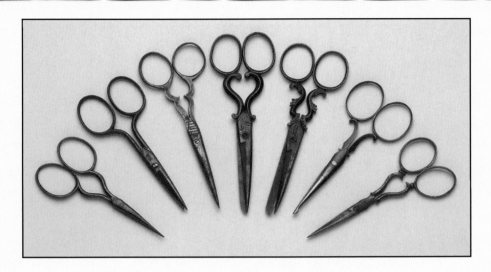

Left to right:
1. USA; steel; embroidery; c. 1875; 3½"; $25.00.
2. Germany; "Hilger & Sons"; plain steel c. 1870; 4"; $20.00.
3. England; cut steel, polished; ribbed design top of blades; c. 1875; 4¼"; $28.00.
4. Germany; gun-metal steel; leaf design top of blades; stamped Blickmand"; c. 1875; 4½"; $35.00.
5. Germany; Butler Bros.; decorative S design; steel; c. 1870; 4½"; $40.00.
6. England; cut, polished steel; tulip design handle; c. 1880; 4"; $24.00.
7. England; cut steel; snake design handle; c. 1800, 4"; $38.00.

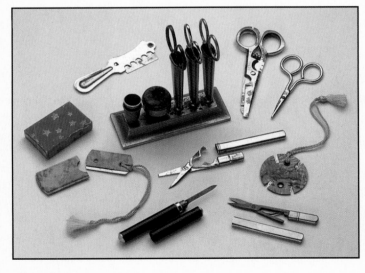

Top row:
1. USA; stainless steel holder; razor blade designed to fit the holder; used for sewing as well as other household projects; c. 1950; 3½"; $7.00.
2. USA; multi-purpose buttonhole scissors; screw size gauge, thread cutter, pattern marker on each handle stamped "Patent Feb. 12, 1901"; "O.K. Universal"; 4½"; $32.00.
3. USA; gilded handles, polished steel blades; c. 1950; 2½"; $13.00.

Row two:
1. USA; celluloid razor blade cutter, storage cover, and original box; c. 1950; 2"; $7.00.
2. Steel scissor caddy; pincushion damaged, thimble and holder, three pairs of scissors; c. 1890; 2" x 3½" x 4½"; $20.00.

Row three:
1. USA; polished steel snips with file and case; stamped "Bes-Gesson"; 3½"; $15.00.
2. USA; plastic disc, razor blade laminated inside, four access slots for use when cutting thread; braid hanger; c. 1950; 1½"; $9.00.

Row four:
1. USA; Bakelite needle case and blade to cut thread; each cover stamped near brass ring in center of case; c. 1920; 4½"; $30.00.
2. Japan; brass handle and case, steel snip; c. 1930; 3¼"; $8.00.

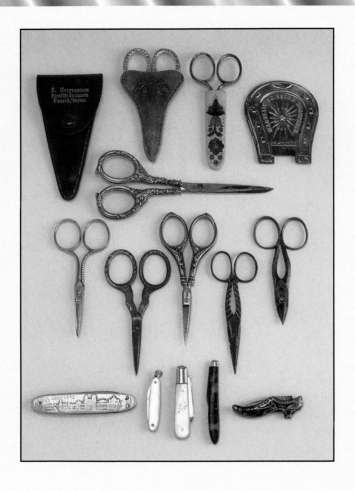

Top row:

Scissors and Sheath

1. Germany: hand-tooled leather lilies and leaves, scissors sterling handles; stamped "J.E. Gladwell Co."; steel blades; $60.00.
2. Germany; leather sheath, snap flap, stamped gold lettering; scissors steel, stamped "I.S. 88 Co." and "D. Morgenstern," "Fuerth/Bayern"; 4½"; $50.00.
3. USA; sheath north European floral designs on heavy paper; steel scissors, stamped "I.S. 88 Co."; and on one blade "Our Very Best"; 4¼"; $38.00.
4. USA; magnetic scissors sharpener; brass and copper; "Pat. app'd for"; 3"; $8.00.

Row two:

Scissors

1. Germany; cut steel, "R.L. Roberts," "Razor" TM; 3¼"; $19.00.
2. Unknown; long handles, short blades, steel; 3½"; $10.00.
3. Unknown; silver plate over steel; beautiful Art Nouveau tropical birds on handles; "Thiers" TM; 4"; $28.00.
4. Unknown; steel, handles bowed; short blades; 3½"; $11.00.
5. Unknown; steel, gilt worn off; 4"; $8.00.

Row three:

Knives

1. Germany; made as a souvenir for the 1893 Columbian Exposition in Chicago, IL; skyline of Exposition on one side, Columbus and dates on other side, "1492, 1892"; 2¾"; $58.00.
2. Mother-of-pearl knife, polished steel single blade; jump ring; 1½"; $12.00.
3. China; decorative mother-of-pearl; England; HM Sheffield, sterling, 1926 knife blade; 2"; $48.00.
4. USA; tortoise shell, one steel blade; 2¼"; $12.00.
5. USA; blackened steel shoe and knife blade, for ladies, a novelty; 1¾"; $10.00.

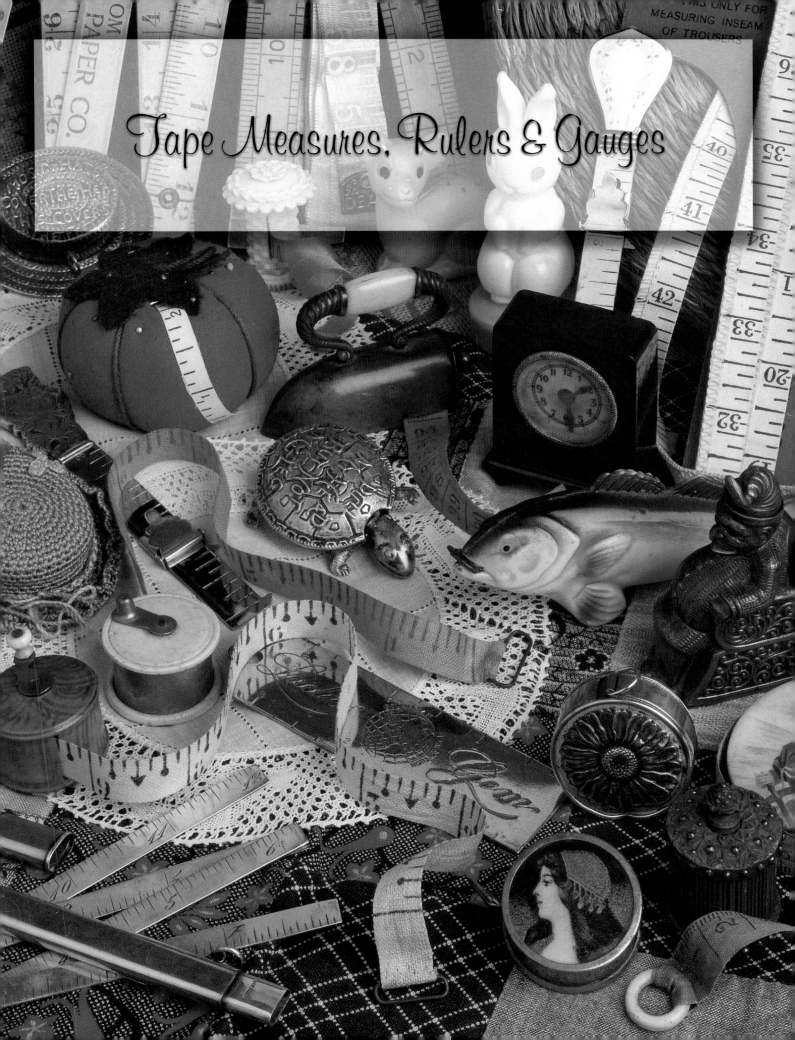

Tape Measures, Rulers & Gauges

Tape Measures, Rulers & Gauges

English households often had a wooden stick as a measure. The sixteenth century "yard stick" was divided in ½, ¼, ⅛, and ⅟₁₆, but not in inches or nails (equivalent of 2¼"). Early nineteenth century tape measures were marked in nails, inches were used later. Early measures were attached to an extended finial, wrapped, and put in a barrel-shaped container. The finial re-wound the measure inside the barrel. The tapes were silk and braid with a metal pull. The standard measuring stick was housed in the local Guildhalls. The spring-return tape measure became available in the late nineteenth century.

There are many styles of figural measures that appeal to collectors. They have been made of many different styles and of many different materials. England, Germany, and Japan have been the major producers of these kinds of tapes; they vary in quality, subject, and finish. They often have country of origin stamped on the tape or the container. Tape measurers were tools for outfitted needlework boxes. Later tape measures were outfitted with metal tapes for durability.

Sewing rulers have ranged in size from four to 36 inches depending on the project. They have been made out of wood, metal, silver, and celluloid. They were used also for advertising. Depending on who the advertiser was has made a number of the rulers very collectible. Hem gauges of four to six inches have been popular because the measuring ease of the size. They often have a "stop" that can be set for the inches needed. The need for different kinds of measuring tools continues to be important and the older ones often continue to be used as well as collected.

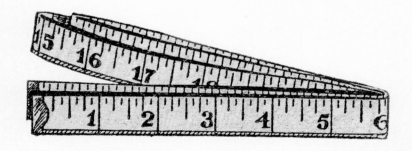

Baltimore Price Reducer, October, 1926.

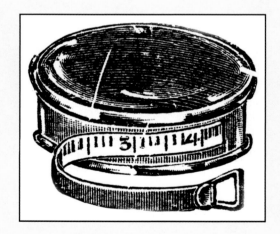

Baltimore Price Reducer, October, 1926.

116

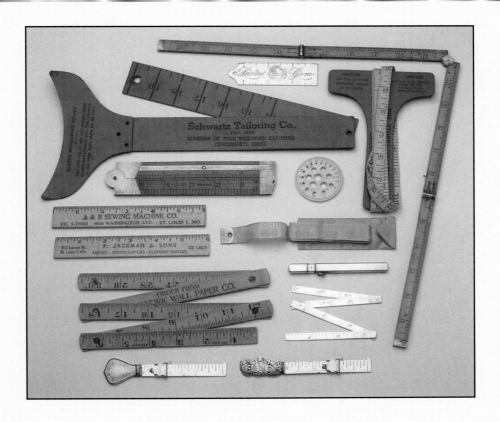

Top row:
1. USA; Stanley wood fold-up ruler, 36", brass hinges and caps; $50.00.

Row two:
1. USA; polished steel 3" rule; "Ladies Gem," globe reads "Columbian Exposition 1893," souvenir, St. Louis, MO; $35.00.

Row three:
1, 2. USA, Cincinnati, Ohio; tailors' measuring device for sleeves and crotch of men's pants; Swartz Tailoring Co.; cardboard; $10.00 each.

Row four:
1. USA; wood fold-up ruler, brass trim, 12", marked "PC 7312" "Boxwood"; $35.00.
2. England; bone disc, knitting needle gage; 24 different sizes can be measured; $38.00.

Row five:
1. USA. St. Louis, MO; 6" wood ruler; "A.B. Sewing Machine Co., 808 Washington Ave."; $8.00.
2. USA, St. Louis, MO; 6" wood ruler; "P. Jackman & Sons," "Fabrics, sewing supplies, cleaners supplies," "21 Locust St."; $800.00.
3. England, London; silk tape measure; handmade silk cover; 1875; $60.00.

Row six:
1. Germany; wood folding ruler, 30"; stamped "order from New York Wallpaper Co."; $75.00.
2. USA; sterling fold-up 12" ruler and case; c. 1920; $75.00.

Row seven:
1. USA; sterling hem gauge, 4", sliding guide; floral enamel over silver top; $80.00.
2. USA; sterling hem gauge, 4", sliding guide; sterling top, large peony and leaves top; c. 1920; $75.00.

Top row:
1. Germany; Bakelite "clock"; arms move around face as tape is in use; c. 1890; $75.00.
2. USA; brass coffee grinder, steel hand crank; cloth tape; c. 1880; $60.00.
3. England; wood barrel; finial hand crank; cloth tape; $50.00.
4. England; painted wood drum; steel hand crank, milk glass knob; c. 1860; $30.00.
5. Japan; celluloid drum; braid trim; cloth tape, some celluloid damage; c. 1930; $25.00.

Row two:
1. England; celluloid drum; wood top and bottom; milk glass knob on hand crank; c. 1890; $30.00.
2. England; beautiful, hand-carved stained wood; carved hand crank; embellished with cut steel beads of several sizes; no tape; c. 1850; $15.00.
3. England; wood gourd; turn finial, cloth tape; c. 1870; $40.00.
4. England; wood column with vegetable ivory overlapping top; cloth tape; c. 1875; $28.00.
5. Japan; bone top and bottom, with rolled steel drum; steel hand crank; cloth tape; $18.00.

Row three:
1. Asia, hand-carved ivory tape holder; pierced carving; silk tape; lacemaking box tool; c. 1850; $80.00.
2. England; layer ivory holder, overlapping top; hand crank; silk tape; c. 1860; $55.00.
3. USA; crochet hat with flowers; tape is stored in crown of hat; c. 1930; $38.00.

118

Top row:
1. USA, Burlington, Iowa; Tri State Fair; spring action; c. 1933; $45.00.
2. USA; Art Deco china head, tape goes in and out her mouth; c. 1920; $62.00.
3. USA; black matte finish, hand-painted flowers and butterfly, spring action; c. 1920; $32.00.

Row two:
1. USA; St. Louis Zoo; advertising; steel and celluloid; c. 1990; $10.00.
2. Germany; sterling silver; large flower on top; spring action; c. 1915; $50.00.
3. USA; celluloid and steel; spring action; c. 1900; $42.00.

Row three:
1. Germany; lady in red hat; steel, spring action; $22.00.
2. Germany; cottage scene; brass box; $20.00.
3. USA; steel flocked to have a leather look; c. 1900; $25.00.

Top row:
1. Germany; celluloid girl in hat with flowers; $65.00.
2. Drum; wood flower garden painted on top; $28.00.
3. Germany; doghouse, dog's head and front legs at the door; $100.00.

Row two:
1. Japan; celluloid, pale strawberry (picked too soon); $50.00.
2. England; hand crank, steel drum, bone disc top & bottom; $28.00.

"She spends hours in the sewing room."

Illustration from *The Mary Frances Sewing Book* by Jane Eayre Fryer.

Celluloid figural tape measures have been produced at a rate faster than baby spiders. They were inexpensive, attractive, and functional. The only real drawback was the life of the spring action of the tape. They have a lot of appeal to collectors because of the many choices, space needed to display, and affordable prices.

Top row:
1. Japan; Florida souvenir; flamingo; $28.00.
2. Standing white rabbit; spring action; $30.00.
3. Japan, dog and puppy on red cushion; $48.00.
4. Japan; fawn; spring action; $28.00.
5. Japan; tomato, cloth felt leaves; spring action; $18.00.
6. Unknown; iron, spring action; celluloid; $35.00.

Row two:
1. Germany; walking bear; rare; spring action; $150.00.
2. Germany; basket of flowers; multicolored; c. 1930; $48.00.
3. Japan; basket of fruit; spring action; c. 1930; $45.00.
4. Pink pig with red hat; c. 1920; $35.00.

Row three:
1. USA, Oklahoma; souvenir; "I was caught at Will Rogers Memorial, Claremore, Okla."; $48.00.

Top row:
1. England; Punch the hat is tape winder; brass; rare; $750.00.
2. "Hat"; nickel-plated brass; "Most hats cover the head this covers the feet"; $200.00.

Row two:
1. "Shoe"; nickel plate over brass; "Three feet-in-one Shoe"; $200.00.
2. "Turtle," nickel-plated brass; "Pull my head not my tail"; $85.00.

Top row:
1. Germany; spring action tape, china girl in yellow dress; $110.00.

Row two:
1. Asia; vegetable ivory drum, cloth tape, ivory finial; $48.00.
2. USA; Stanley, wood and brass ruler, 5"; $35.00.

Row three:
1. Germany; celluloid top, steel case, retrieve button, braid tape; 1" square; $45.00.
2. USA; celluloid advertising ruler, 1919 calendar on back; $4.00.

Mauchline, Tartan & Tunbridge Ware

The manufacture of Mauchline ware was begun by William and Andrew Smith in the early 1800s and continued until a fire in the 1930s ended production. Their factory was known as the Box Works and located in Mauchline, Ayshire, Scotland. It was also the home of the famous Scottish poet, Robert Burns.

John Sandy invented the "hidden hinge" snuff box. The importance of this durable design is the fact that hinges are still in good working order today. The first manufacturer after Sandy's death was William Crawford in 1810.

By 1820 there were fifty manufacturers in the Ayrshire area making snuff boxes. When the demand for snuff boxes declined, a number of the factories closed. W. and A. Smith's Box Works survived because of their diversification, "from a stamp box to tea trays," quoting Andrew Smith in the *Art Journal*. The wood of choice was sycamore because of the fine grain and color.

The boxes were decorated with hand-painted images on wood, then scenes painted on paper glued to surface and varnished. In the 1880s, etchings and steel engravings were transferred on tops and sides of the items. These were made for the tourist trade and were found at the site of the transfers. The largest group of items produced were for needlework. A large number of manufacturers of thread, ribbon, string, pins, and needles ordered boxes to house their products and had their trademark label placed on the top and/or inside the box. Two of the well-known thread companies were J and P Coats and Clark's. The Caledonian Box Works produced a large number of thread boxes for J and P Coats and other thread companies. Spindles were secured in the boxes and bone eyelets in the sides to minimize a tangle of threads. The transfers represent not only sites in Great Britain but also France, Germany, Italy, and USA.

Tartanware

Tartanware was wood based and early items were hand-painted clan plaids. W. and A. Smith designed a machine that could "weave" tartan designs on paper in 1850. Each tartan design was stamped in gold lettering with the name of the clan. Two other factories made tartanware, Davidson Wilson and Amulet, and Archibald Brown's Caledonian Box Works, from the 1860s.

Fernware

Fernware was manufactured by W. and A. Smith from 1900 to 1930. Live ferns were used during early production. When costs became a factor, the fern images were outlined and color added. John Baker writes that "in most cases real ferns were used for small sewing items as well as large items such as chests and beds." Fernware was considered gift items and not souvenirs.

The three rows of Mauchline ware represent various uses, subjects, shapes, and sizes; made in Scotland. Sycamore was the wood of choice for a long time.

Top row:
1. Box for storing small items; decal of etching The Pier Weston Super Mare; thimble, punch, thread, pins, and needles; c. 1900; $65.00.
2 – 5. Etching transferred to wood, then varnished; thread boxes.
    2. Label inside lid "J and P Coats Cord"; etching of USS Vesuvius in active service 1890 – 1921, member of fleet during Spanish American War off of Cuba; built at yard in Philadelphia, Pa., sold for scrap 1922; collection item; $350.00.
    3. Etching of Isle of Wight; 2" x 4" x 5"; $150.00.
    4. Label "J and P Coats Best Six Cord"; etching transfer Mirror Lake and Lake Placid, NY; Redditch, England, Needles; 2¼" x 3½" x 5"; $98.00.
    5. Label "Use Clark's ONT, Geo. Clark sole agent"; bone eyelets for thread; $310.00.

Row two:
1, 2, 3, 5. Etching transfer then coats of varnish.
    1. Box top etching transfer Melrose Abbey; "Grown on the lands of Abbotsford"; spindles and eyelets for thread, thimble holder, three etching transfers on sides, Abbotsford Floor Castle, Dryburg Abbey; 2" x 4"; $260.00.
    2. Thread and string holder, released through the top for continuous work such as knitting or crochet; braid hanger; etching transfer Pevensey Castle; 4" x 4"; $100.00.
    3. Needle and pin holder; etching transfers on side Il Fracombe and Capstone Hill Parade; on the top Watermouth Cave, Il Fracombe; 1½" x 3"; $89.00.
4. Black painted wood box; four spindles and bone eyelets; portrait of Queen Victoria paper decal transfer; 1877; $300.00.
5. Round thread holder, bone eyelet; etching transfer, paper decal; The Pier Eastbourne; 2" x 3½"; $95.00.

Row three:
1. Wood thread box, sides with decorative paper covering; top, a scene of Victorian children dressed like adults, at tea; label inside "Clark's Spool Cotton" F. Mark sole agent; c. 1880; $210.00.
2. Wood box, cat and mouse watching each other; hook catch; paper advertising labels inside and on bottom, Brook's Thread; 3½" x 4"; $225.00.
3. Photo paper decal on top of black painted wood box; brass fittings; photo: "Great Eastern," "Largest Steamship in the World, length 698 ft., breadth 83 ft., tonnage 22,927 tons, Registration 18,914 tons"; label inside "Clark and Co's Anchor Sewing Cotton, Best for hand machine use," black and red anchor; collection item; $500.00.

Each Mauchline item in the photo has etchings transferred on raw wood then coated with varnish. These items represent a lot of different designs and uses.

Top row:
1. Thimble holder and thimble, red lining, brass catch and hinge, image is Dover Castle; 1" x 1½"; $160.00.
2. Stamp box, two slanted slots inside; transfer Harriet Beecher Stowe House, Brunwick, ME; 2" x 2½"; $75.00.
3. Stamp box with slanted slots; holds more than #2; transfer Wolfeboro N.H., from the Lake; 2" x 3"; $60.00.
4. Display box; many uses; transfer Windsor Castle and Channel; $65.00.
5. Stool with pinkeep seat; transfer Dunoon from Church tower; $75.00.
6. Caldron with ball feet; pincushion; transfer Beachyhead Lighthouse; $72.00.

Row two:
1. Needle book, two wool pages, ribbon hanger; two transfers, Caresbrooke Castle and Ventor Looking West; 2" x 3½"; $100.00.
2. Large needle book, two wool pages for needles; transfer, Burns Cottage and one of his poems; this item was purchased at his cottage; the town is the location of the early Mauchline factory, The Box Works; $110.00.
3. Whistle, they were popular with women; transfer The Summit House Wachusett Mountain, Mass. 2018 feet above sea level; 3"; $45.00.
4. Bell-shaped tape measure, blue silk tape; transfer The Exe, Triverton; knob turns tape; 2"; $65.00.
5. School bell tape measure; handle turns tape; Porchester Castle; $165.00.
6. Egg-shaped sewing kit; thimble, pins, needles, thread; transfer Killiechassie Beach; 3"; $65.00.
7. Small egg-shaped sewing kit; thread, needles, thimble; The Flume, Franconia Notch, NH; 2½"; $75.00.

Row three:
1, 2, 4, 5. These are four round pinkeeps, slightly different sizes and different transfers.
    1. Kennebunk Beach; 1¾"; $85.00.
    2. Bird's Eye View of World's Fair Columbian Exposition, Chicago, 1893; 1½"; $150.00.
3. Diamond shape, one straight end; The Toll Booth Old Edinburgh; 1½"; $120.00.
    4. Flamborough Lighthouse; on back The Storm a Bridlington Quay; 2"; $110.00.
    5. Summit of Mt. Washington; 1¼"; $90.00.

Row four:
1. Knitting needle case, four steel, 6½" needles; Sandown Bay; 9½"; $125.00.
2. Beading needle case; Cambridge Chapel; 3½"; $90.00.

Top row:

Tartan ware is wood items wrapped with paper printed with an individual clan tartan.
1 – 6. Tartan ware.

1. Egg sewing kit; decorated with gold braid; Prince Charles tartan; 2"; $175.00.
2. Needle case; McBeth tartan; 2"; $150.00.
3. Ribbon dispenser; McBeth tartan; 2½"; $250.00.
4. Beehive yarn and string holder on a base; Prince Charles tartan; 2½"; $175.00.
5. Needle case; McBeth tartan; $98.00.
6. Tatting shuttle; MacDonald tartan; $140.00.

Row two:

During the first quarter of the nineteenth century, Tunbridge Wells woodworkers developed an end-grain mosaic by gluing small hardwood sticks of different colors, making a circular or rectangular block. The mosaic design was visible at the end and went through the length of the block allowing very thin cuts. This technique was much less expensive than inlay and allowed for a large variety of patterns. Stickware blocks were turned on a lathe leaving a more open linear design.

1, 2, 3, 5. End-grain mosaic.
1. Needle book, wool pages for needles; mosaic floral design on front and back; 1½" x 2½"; $100.00.
2. Mosaic top and sides, tape measure; $110.00.
3. Barrel thimble holder, mosaic top; $75.00.
5. Mosaic top, stamp box; 2½"; $70.00.

4, 6, 7. Stickware lathe cut.
4. Germany; ball darner; 2"; $85.00.
6. Acorn thimble holder, stickware top; inscribed "Prescont from the Tunnel"; $100.00.
7. Pincushion and waxer, stick ware top and stand; $68.00.

Row three:

Production of Fernware decorative items began as early as 1870. Although W & A Smith of The Box Works were the first producers, the Caledonian Box Works in Lanark introduced their own Fernware products. The different color techniques gave each manufacturer their own identity. Real ferns used in the transfer process were applied to the raw wood, then the long slow application and drying of layers of varnish. The difference between Mauchline and Fern ware was fern ware were considered gifts not souvenirs.

Left to right:
1. Three-spool thread holder, bone thread release in top; fern painted green; 3½"; $100.00.
2. Clover-shaped pinkeep, tan fern on brown background, greeting on back; $110.00.
3. Tatting shuttle, painted fern red and green; $90.00.
4. Needlebook; felt needle pages; ferns & flowers; $110.00.
5. Tatting shuttle; dark stain with tan fern; $95.00.
6. Heart-shaped pinkeep; green and brown painted fern; etching transfer The Alexandra Palace; $130.00.
7. Painted transfer, bouquet of colorful flowers on a table; needle and pin holder with ivory marker, silk lining; c. 1877; $210.00.

Mauchline

1. Needle book, etching transfer of Crawford House; cotton and velvet lining, good condition; 4"; $75.00.
2. Tear drop sewing kit; cylinder for wrapping thread and hollow for needles; etching transfer Il Fracombe from Hillsborough; 2½"; $70.00.
3. Thread holder, slit for thread release; large impressive etching transfer of Wallace Monument on Abbey Craig; made of wood which grew on the Abbey Craig, the site of the National Wallace Monument; 2½"; $145.00.
4. Pincushion, velvet; etching of Radcliff Library, Oxford; 2"; $58.00.

Tunbridge

Lady's powder box represents the beautiful simplicity of some Tunbridge items. This would, possibly, have been one piece of a dresser set, used for traveling.

Tartan Ware

1. Thread box; McPherson plaid; J. & P. Coats thread company label inside box top; five spools of thread; tartan paper at edges beginning to break off; 3½" x 5"; $50.00.
2. Double-end pincushion; Cameron plaid; good condition; 1½"; $60.00.

Chatelaines & Accessories

Gay Ann Rogers writes that early Victorian chatelaines were steel and made in Birmingham by the steel toymakers. Toymaker often referred to the maker of a lot of household items of polished iron and steel. The late 1800s brought about a new rise in the popularity of chatelaines; they became ornate and less functional. Sewing tools were still available and sometimes seen with art tools on same chatelaine. The most popular had three to seven chains, although they were available with one or two chains. There were also doll chatelaines for girls. Chatelaines were made of many different materials, the most durable being the metal ones. During the 1920s and 1930s ribbon chatelaines became popular and were often handmade by the owner. They were a combination of silk ribbon and bone rings that made the chains and multiple loop bows to take the place of a clasp and attached to the clothing with a safety pin. The tool holders were often made by the owner, such as a thimble holder, needlebook, pincushion, and sheath for scissors. They were also commercially made.

The fine chatelaines of iron, steel, silver, and gold are difficult to find. They are often being made of bits and parts from old chatelaines and sold for original at antique prices. So, once again "buyer beware."

Germany; ironwork filigree; belt clip; five chains, medallion clip decorated with eight round, black glass settings and four oval; filigree ribbon set with three lines of four oval black glass settings, one round; each tool chain has a round black glass set at the top of the chain; tools include pencil with slide, tablet, scissors sheath, pinkeep, thimble bucket; each tool has two glass sets oval in shape; excellent condition; c. 1800; 2½" x 14"; $2,300.00.

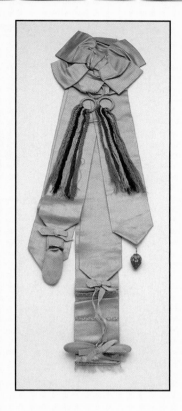

USA; handmade satin ribbon chatelaine; safety pin behind large bow for attaching to blouse or waist; three tool ribbons; near bow braided sewing thread hanging from bone rings, thimble holder and thimble, needle book wool pages, glove darner, small emery; $150.00.

Clockwise:
1. England; chatelaine, five filigree chains, no tools; open-work medallion clip with winged Cupid; c. 1875; $450.00.
2. USA; Simons Bros. Co., sterling thimble; decorative silver thimble bucket; c. 1900; 1¼" x ¾"; $125.00.
3. USA; sterling acorn thimble holder with decorative hinged top; monogram "P.L. T."; c. 1910; 3" x ½"; $110.00.
4. England; needle holder, open end; repoussé leaves; blue leather insert to hold needles; c. 1900; 3" x ½"; $90.00.
5. USA; sterling needle holder, open end; repoussé flowers and leaves; c. 1900; 3" x 1"; $95.00.
6. USA; R & B CO.; plain sterling needle holder; c. 1915; 3"; $65.00.
7. Northern Europe; nickel silver pinkeep, decorative flowers and profiles; c. 1915; $25.00.
8. USA; F & B; sterling capped red fabric strawberry emery; c. 1910; $87.00.
9. England; .800 silver acorn perfume holder lined with cork; c. 1870; 1¼"; $70.00.
10. USA; sterling ribbed pencil holder with red stone mounting; flat wood lead pencil; c. 1900; 2"; $28.00.
11. England; sterling needle case; repoussé flowers; c. 1900; $60.00.
12. USA; sterling stamp holder; fan and fern designs, monogram "A"; c. 1900; 1¼" x 1"; $125.00.
13. USA; sterling needle case, leaf designs; stores sizes 5 – 9 needles, holes according to size releases needles; c. 1890; $95.00.
14. USA; sterling capped, acorn emery; shammy cover; c. 1890; 1" x 1"; $50.00.
15. USA; sterling walnut emery pincushion; c. 1920; 1¼" x 1"; $55.00.
16. USA; sterling pinkeep; pink silk ribbon; joined layers by hand stitch; c. 1860; 1"; $60.00.
17. USA; sterling ladies round, mesh purse, "P.E. .925"; decorative medallion; used for carrying handkerchief, coins, or other small items; c. 1900; $150.00.
18. USA; sterling capped ear of corn waxer; pointed cap; c. 1900; 2" x 3"; $100.00.
19. USA; silver-plated pinkeep with handle; primitive figure in medallion, border of masks; c. 1875; 1½" x 1"; $65.00.

Top row:

1. USA; acorn, shammy covered emery, sterling cap with ring; c. 1890; 1" x 1"; $50.00.
2. England; very decorative set, matching scissors and sheath; eyelets on side of handles, making the set wearable on chatelaine or with a necklace chain; c. 1860; 6"; $180.00.
3. France; steel scissors; silver sheath with niello designs, applied decorative metal work; two sizes of chain; c. 1850; 6½"; $150.00.
4. England; two-piece sterling bucket with handle and catch; sterling thimble; ornate floral design; 1885; 2"; $160.00.
5. France; silver-plated tablet and wood pencil; decorative top and left hand corner; applied fleur de lis; disc of Mont St. Michel, flowers on back; c. 1910; 2" x 1¼"; $55.00.

Row two:

1. USA; thread waxer, dyed red beeswax; sterling cap; scalloped beaded rim; c. 1890; 1⅜"; $75.00.
2. USA; sterling emery cap, decorative scalloped rim; printed cotton fabric; F & B; c. 1900; 2¼"; $110.00.

Row three:

1. USA; sterling needle case; monogram "F.G. B."; c. 1920; 3"; $70.00.
2. England; pomander, .800 silver, cap has holes to release fragrance; "Cagy" monogram; bright work; c. 1850; 2" x 1½"; $125.00.
3. USA; sterling peanut, red pincushion; c. 1900; 1½"; $42.00.

Row four:

1. USA; Simons Bros. Co, Philadelphia, PA; sterling pencil and case; wood, lead pencil, "Mable, Todd & Co."; c. 1915; 3"; $55.00.
2. England; HM Chester; sterling, 1913; monogram "W.J.E."; geometric pattern, pencil slide; wood, lead pencil, Mordan & Co.; 3"; $75.00.

Row five:

1. USA; sterling travel mirror; cartouche and ribbing on back; c. 1920; 2½"; $30.00.
2. USA; sterling buttonhook; used for clothing made of fine, lightweight fabrics; decorative applied coral and agate ovals; made by Clark; c. 1910; 2¾"; $28.00.
3. USA; sterling handle, mother-of-pearl blade letter opener; decorative beading; c. 1905; 2¼"; $28.00.
4. Southeast Asia; reproduction; sterling floral design needle holder; copy of nineteenth century English item; c. 1995; 3"; $35.00.
5. USA; Avon whistle, silver plate; reproduction; c. 1985; 1½" x ½"; $12.00.

The long linked chain made it possible to use tools without removing them from the chains. The cut steel pieces were more popular than precious metal during the 18th century. The workmanship was outstanding in its complex simplicity. Chatelaine popularity waned after 1840 but the Victorian clothing styles created renewed interest. They became much more ornate and also became more specialized such as the sewing chatelaines. It is common for the tools not to match because manufacturers made many different tools to fit the same set of chains. If a chatelaine has a matching set of tools and waist clip, expect it to be expensive.

Three cut steel chatelaines, small decorative medallions.
1. Gun metal finish; five chains and four tools, a ball tape measure, acorns pinkeep, scissors, thimble bucket; $250.00.
2. Polished steel; three long chains; two half chains; these chains are a combination of long and short links; tools; thimble bucket (only original piece), sovereign coin holder, folding iron corkscrew, folding button hook; $300.00.
3. Polished cut steel; four long chains and four tools original; thimble bucket, scissors, needle case, and acorn pinkeep; $450.00.

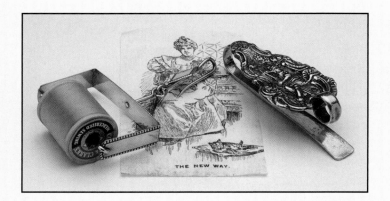

1. Chatelaine for continuous work such as knitting, crochet, tatting; called the New Way; it has a vertical pin to attach to garment; decorative beading on rim of thread holder; 1890; $100.00.
2. Netherlands; chatelaine clip, holds one item, umbrella, drawing box; sterling HM; $125.00.

Chatelaine of coins; large coin in center of clip 1887; five gold coins, profile Georgius Rex, lions on back; one coin profile of Victoria with crown 1887, twenty-five coins issued 1834, 1838, 1839, 1841, 1862, 1887; "Victoria de Brittania Regina"; five chains; very unusual, of interest for a number of different kinds of collectors; collection item; NPA.

These chatelaines and accessories are from China; they are .800 silver; and were used when men and women wore kimonos.
1. Men's; top in shape of fan houses belt clip; tools: ear wax spoon, tweezers, toothpick; 12"; $500.00.
2. Men's needle case, chain drops down to load and unload needles; 1875; 2½"; $65.00.
3. Ornate needle case; complex repoussé design; 1850; 3"; $50.00.
4. Ladies' chatelaine, thin belt clip; tools hang from middle of chatelaine, toothpick, ear wax spoon; interesting decorative pieces; c. 1860; 18"; $400.00.

These ribbon chatelaines were made in the USA during the 1920s and 1930s. Although they are not as elegant as the silver and other metals, they are attractive and show talent with a low budget item. Using bright silk, each one creates a delighted reaction. A safety pin attached for wearing.

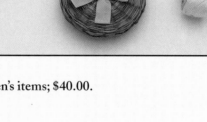

1. Red ribbon woven through bone rings; tools: scissors, ribbon-edged needle book, red strawberry emery; $22.00.
2. Yellow silk ribbon is attached to each sweet grass tool by hand, needle book, scissors in sheath, round needle book, thimble holder; $50.00.
3. Gold silk ribbon woven with bone rings adds a different style with double bows; tools are buttonhole scissors, two spools darning thread, and a painted darner for children's items; $40.00.

Top row:
1. France; decorative sheath with original scissors; applied open work to sheath includes hearts touching; gilded; c. 1850; $125.00.
2. France; gold sheath original scissors; beautiful, complex ornamentation; c. 1850; $140.00.

Row two:
1. Germany; gilded silver, four chain chatelaine clip with medallion shield border of flying dragons; two items: small claw with silver ring fetish and perfume bottle; "str. . 925"; $250.00.
2. USA; sterling, stylized butterfly; four chains, sterling; vinegarette with holes in top, tablet, compact, purse, pencil retractable; c. 1900; $550.00.

Row three:
1. England; open worn pin; five chains, four accessories: compact, needlecase, pencil, fob; monogram "C"; c. 1900; $400.00.

England; three-piece base metal pharaoh head soldered on clasp; thimble bucket, scissor sheath, and pinkeep; a make-do of old parts, poorly constructed; $150.00.

These chatelaine accessories were part of a collection representing three generations of a New England family. Some of their more traditional items are missing, such as thimble holder, scissors, and notebook. The collection is very interesting in its diversity.

All the tools hung individually at the end of black silk ribbon, suspended from a sterling bangle. A good idea to prevent misplacing one or all the tools when stored away.

Top row:
1. USA; Art Nouveau decorative design; sterling; card holder that was converted to a scissors holder; monogram "LER"; c. 1905; 2¾" x 1½"; $100.00.
2. USA; emery, sterling cap, shammy cover badly worn; c. 1900; 1" x 1"; $45.00.
3. USA; needle case, swing arm; filled with early needles; c. 1891; ¾" x 3"; $40.00.
4. USA; open end needle case; ¾" x 3"; c. 1900; $50.00.
5. Perfume with sterling mounting with chain; glass bottle and stopper, chipped; c. 1890; $200.00.

Row 2:
1. USA; sterling pencil, screw lead release; ornate design; 3"; $25.00.
2. USA; sterling handle, steel punch; 4"; $40.00.
3. USA; four arm silk thread winder, ornate; 2"; $98.00.
4. USA; sterling, four, squared arm, silk winder; 2"; $110.00.
5. USA; sterling capped thread waxer, yellow dye; 1½"; $75.00.
6. China; open thimble, metal, 1" long; $25.00.
7. USA; three sterling bodkins, each for different size of ribbon; $20.00 – 50.00 each.

Sewing Tools: Representative Items of Collections

The generosity of sewing tool collectors resulted in a collection chapter. Each collector has selected tools that represent their interest. Some are individuals that have been collectors for a number of years; some are fairly new collectors. There are some collections with limited price guides that do not take away the pleasure of seeing items that are unusual and/or rare. There are many variations of the most ordinary tools and the more complex.

NC – The collector of dog and cat pincushions has a delightful sense of humor, and represent her love of animals; assorted pieces page 54, 55; lovely dolls page 53; page 61, 125.

KY – The nineteenth century Japanese sewing box was made for the more affluent households. This is the centerpiece of the collector's sewing tools, page 22.

IL – The barnyard caddies are on display in the collector's study/workroom and other pieces are in glass cases for enjoyment in their living and dining rooms, page 16.

MO – These nineteenth century souvenir sailboat thimble holders are items that interest individuals with a diversity of tools. These boats introduced a beginning collector to thimble holders, page 83.

MO – Interest in small thread holders and accessories grew out of "space available" with a growing family. Occasionally a larger piece will join the smalls. Chapter 5, page 90, center, the desk thread stand, made by Frye.

MO – The collector has an outstanding collection with thimbles and accessories as the central focus.

The dates span seven centuries. The wall displays are organized for easy viewing, outstanding representative item – one of many, page 71 – 73, 83.

PA – It is interesting to note the variety of handouts that were made for women 100 years before they could vote and up to the present day. The collectors enjoy their collection with their favorite pieces displayed for their pleasure, page 139 – 142.

NH – An antique New England desk with glass doors houses this small but interesting group of handmade pieces, page 138.

NH – A built-in shelf wall unit with glass sliding doors houses an interesting selection of early Shaker and New England sewing tools. The display is in the home office of the collector, page 143 – 145.

NH – This beautifully woven Shaker yarn holder adorns an early Shaker side table in the collector's office. Chapter 5, page 91.

MA – There are displays in upright and flat glass top cases that allow friends interested in sewing tools a visual treat. The flat cases make it more convenient to rotate displays when a change is wanted or if there is a loan request for an exhibit. Husband and wife enjoyed the "seek and find" with their collection hunting, page 155 – 158.

TN – The collector's husband has built beautiful display cabinets and shelving for the sewing tools. There are informal displays also. She started with kitchen tools and sewing machines, soon the "ripple effect" took over with complementary acquisitions, page 148 – 154.

Top row:
1. USA; handmade pincushion; bird tree make-do with leaded glass, wine glass base; small round pincushion on top; variety of fabrics, some worn; c. 1880; 6" x 7½"; $25.00.
2. Germany; celluloid and brass tape measure; photo Diana's Bath, North Conway; c. 1920; 1¾"; $35.00.

Row two:
1. USA; White Mts., New Hampshire; roll up, cotton print, silk binding; two pockets storing hexagon pattern, two packets of needles "WC Crowley & Sons, John English & Co., Great Britain 1863; red wool pages for loose needles; $75.00.
2. USA; wool felt glove needle book; packet of needles H. Baylis, England; decorative stitching, mother-of-pearl button; $10.00.
3. England; knitting needle guards; leather, silk cuffs; joined with braid; handmade; c. 1900; $25.00.
4. Germany; tape measure, red celluloid, brass trim, spring action; c. 1920; ½" x 1"; $30.00.

USA, New England; sewing box; handmade wood; hinged top, three bone eyelets for thread release; lower area contains spools of silk and cotton thread, small leather pincushion, worn leather pinkeep; "Rice's Sewing Silk, Pittsfield, Mass, USA"; top tray has assorted mother-of-pearl buttons, silk thread "Eureka Silk Mfr. Co, Est. 1840," two "Redi-End Pure Silk made in USA," darning thread, and needles; $65.00.

Political and Campaign Sewing Tools

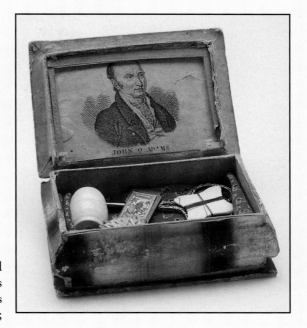

John Quincy Adams sewing box; top cushion, "Adams Forever" and flags, portrait of Adams inside cover, box made of papier mache; tools in box from fourth quarter of nineteenth century; John Quincy Adams served two terms, 1844 – 1852, as president; 4¾"l x 3½" w x 2½"h; NPA.

1. Henry Clay rare handmade pinkeep for 1844 campaign, lithograph paper portrait of Clay; pinkeep made of silk and cardboard; Clay served as senator from Kentucky and ran for president three times; NPA.
2. Scotland; Mauchline pinkeep; etching of white House transfer on sycamore wood, mirror on back; $100.00.
3. Scotland; Mauchline thread box; ONT Clark's, label inside lid "George A. Clark, sole agent"; ⅔rd portrait of Lincoln and facsimile of handwriting, steel engraving transfer on box top; Lincoln elected as president 1860 and 1864, shot in 1865 by John Wilkes Booth; this may have been a Bicentennial souvenir; $700.00.

1. USA; F & K Yarn Co., NYC, 1912, "the yarn with a reputation for 30 years"; Theodore Roosevelt paper label wrapping two spools of silk gimp (decorative braid); $10.00 each.
2. Plastic thimbles, campaign souvenirs.
   Red; $5.00.
   Pat Nixon, "Pat for First Lady"; $25.00.
   1940, Windell Wilkie for president, Kent Co. Women's Club; $18.00.
   1988, Jessie Jackson, Democrat, primary election; $5.00.
   1992, Bill Clinton – Al Gore Elect leadership, vote Democratic; $5.00.
   1988, Robert Dole Republican, "vote for Dole for president"; primary election; $4.00.
   1948, Harry Truman & Alben Barkley Democrat "sew right with Harry," compliments of MO. State Dem Com.; $24.00.
   1976, Jimmy Carter, Democrat, Jimmy Carter for president in '76; $5.00.
   1960, John F. Kennedy Democrat; $8.00.
   1924, Robert La Follette & Burton Wheeler, Populist party; aluminum; $75.00 – 90.00.
   1924, Calvin Coolidge & Charles Dawes Republican party; aluminum; $75.00 – 90.00.
   1936, Alfred M. Landon & Frank Knox Republican party; two aluminum whistles; $50.00.
   1928, Herbert Hoover & Charles Curtis Republican; $14.00.
   1984, Ronald Reagan & George Bush Republican; $30.00.
3. Sewing kit; 1952, Dwight Eisenhower & Richard Nixon; "Let's Sew it up for Ike and Dick, vote Republican"; $40.00.
4 – 6. Souvenir scissors with presidential medallions.
   4. 1904, Theodore Roosevelt on front with floral design, Edith Roosevelt on back of handle; $100.00.
   5. 1908, oval portrait of William Howard Taft and Mrs. Helen Taft; $50.00.
   6. 1922, Woodrow Wilson and Lady Liberty; Democrat; $50.00.

Top row:
1. Sarah's Suffrage Victory Campaign Fund thread holder; holds spools of thread 40, 50, 60 and has dispensing openings; manufacturer Thread Holder Co., Boston, Mass; note additional information in a copy of ad for it in 1915 suffrage newspaper; NPA.
2. Grover and Frances Cleveland shopping for fabric, Gilbert Mfg. Co., dress linen dept. color advertising card; Gover saying "my dear"; $30.00.
3. 1892; Grover Cleveland & Adlai Stevenson, Democrat; blue ribbon chenille flower; compliments of Singer Mfg. Co.; $70.00.

Row two:
1. 1910 – 1920; Pennsylvania senator C. Wm. Beales pictured on tape measure, campaign item; $25.00.
2. 1940; crochet brimmed hat, Wilkie embroidered on brim; Wendell Wilkie & Charles McNary, Republican; $18.00.
3. 1940; Wendell Wilkie & Charles McNary, Republican, defeated by Franklin Roosevelt for president; campaign handout a match book, Wilkie portrait in front of NY keystone; $12.00.

Row three:
1. 1904; Theodore Roosevelt & Charles Fairbanks, Republican; celluloid covered tape measure; pair in photo, capitol building on reverse; sepia; $125.00.

Row four:
1. 1892; Frances Cleveland; lithograph on tin portrait and name on front; compliments of Garland Stoves; $34.00.
2. Wm. Howard Taft medallion on package of "Taft Sharps Needles"; made in Germany; $10.00.
3. Grover Cleveland and Frances entwined in thread heart with two little putti; "the thread that binds the Union"; Merrick Thread Co., in color; $25.00.

Top row:
1. 1884; Grover Cleveland, Democrat & James Blaine, Republican; booklet in color; information included calendar, electoral votes, presidents list; Kerr's Spool Cotton sponsor; $45.00.
2. 1928; Herbert Hoover & Charles Curtis on front of folder, slogans "Vote for Republican Party and Prosperity," inside slate of candidates; $15.00.

Row two:
1. 1888; Benjamin Harrison & Levi Morton, Republican; compliments of "Eclipse Sewing Machine Co., Cincinnati, Ohio"; $15.00.
2. James Blain & John Logan Republican; sponsor "The Old Reliable Singer Co. Cleveland, Ohio"; $15.00.

Row three:
1. James Blain & Grover Cleveland multiple portraits; Belding Thread Co., large card with election information on back; $20.00.
2. 1892; Frances Cleveland seated at "Household Sewing Machine" manufactured in Providence, RI; political and commercial advertising card; Grover standing behind Frances; $25.00.
3. 1884; Grover Cleveland card sponsor "buy the New Arn Davis Sewing Machine"; $20.00.

1. 1908; political pincushion postcards, opposing candidates; red, white, and blue; primary caricature; William Howard Taft, Republican; with stuffed belly with political fabric; on right a drawing of a gun boat, on left the White House; "Big enough to fill the White House"; $100.00.
2. Theodore Roosevelt, Republican; Big stick stuffed with cotton and covered with political fabric; multicolored; to left small caricature of Taft; "Me and my people"; cartoonish L.H. Sykes, presidential series; $100.00.

A collection of interesting Shaker and New England items.

Top row, left to right:
1. USA, New England; beautiful Canterbury Shaker, woven box wide satin ribbon woven into lid; details below.
2. USA; small strawberry of pink satin and velvet with silk hanger; $45.00.
3. USA, New England; turned wood sewing stand; pink velvet pincushion with plastic thimble, hanging emery velvet and satin, and needle book with wool pages, five spindles, two spools of thread; early 20th century; $110.00.

Row two:
1. USA, New England; pincushion roll; yellow, red, tan woven fabric strips embroidered together; fringe at ends; 3½"; $38.00.
2. USA, New England; silk ribbon reel; floral print fabric covers cardboard ends; 3½"; $42.00.
3. USA; large print fabric pincushion; satin ribbon on corner; glass head and steel pins arranged in attractive triangles; 6" x 9½"; $48.00.

Row three:
1. USA; pie-shaped beeswax with silk ribbon hanger; $10.00.
2. USA; small woven basket velvet pincushion; Shaker; leather trim; floral painting on bottom; 1½" x 2"; $50.00.
3. USA; three-piece silk ribbon chatelaine; heart-shaped pincushion; silk emery, needle, and pin book; $70.00.
4. USA; candle-shaped beeswax with hanger; 1"; $7.00.

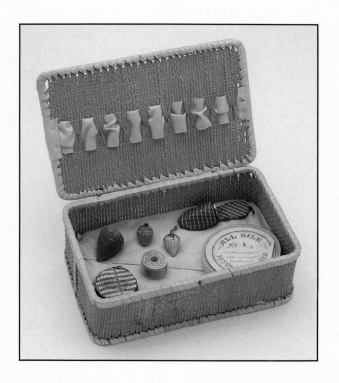

Woven Shaker box with leather trim; silk covered padding pillow; contents: one large, two small emeries, stripe silk pinkeep, small spool silk thread, reel of silk ribbon, checked silk slipper thimble holder, silver thimble; c. 1920; 8" x 2" x 5"; $325.00.

Top row:
1. USA; red and tan silk checkerboard pincushion; corner ribbon trim; 4"; $35.00.
2. USA; Shaker woven basket, leather trim, red velvet pincushion, ribbon trim; floral painting on bottom; 1½" x 2"; $50.00.
3. USA; Shaker blue silk pincushion with small waxer and emery attached; $38.00.
4. Pig tape measure; base metal gilded; tail turns to retrieve the cloth tape; c. 1880; $75.00.

Row two:
1. USA; plastic tatting shuttle; $15.00.
2. USA; silk ribbon with worn emery; $18.00.

Row three:
1. USA; small two-piece silk ribbon chatelaine; heart-shaped pincushion, fabric pin, and needle book; early twentieth century; $48.00.
2. USA; crochet hooks, two ivory, three bone, one bone punch; $3.00 – 8.00 each.
3. China; ivory silk thread winder; may have been a tool in a lacemaking box; $30.00.

Top row, left to right:
1. USA; Corticelli silk thread; small spool, blue; $2.00.
2. USA; Shaker woven basket with leather trim, navy velvet pincushion, c. early twentieth century; 1½" x 2"; $40.00.
3. USA; oak splits basket with lower pieces dyed navy; navy blue velvet pincushion; $48.00.
4. USA; Canterbury, New Hampshire; Shaker village; spool keep, navy leather and silk ribbon; access to thread without removing spool; three different spool sizes; early twentieth century; $200.00.

Row two:
1. USA; corticelli silk thread; $2.00; plastic thimble; $7.50.
2. USA; cotton canvas fabric scissors sheath; portrait transfer, black and white; drawing of scissors; c. 1910; $45.00.
3. USA; Shaker blue silk ribbon chatelaine; ribbon threaded on bone rings, two large bows top one has safety pin for attaching to garment; six tools: brass thimble, painted darner for small work, darner with handle, strawberry emery; ribbon bodkin, ivory punch. c. 1920; $210.00.
4. USA; small sweet grass basket pincushion; $35.00.
5. USA; Shaker white silk ribbon, three-piece chatelaine; ribbon threaded on bone rings; small heart-shaped emery, ivory punch, brass thimble; c. 1920; $65.00.

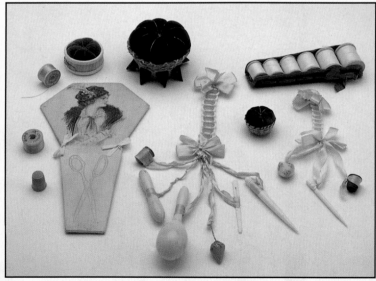

Top row:
1. USA; beautiful floral silk print cover pincushion; satin ribbon on corner; c. 1920; $38.00.
2. USA; silk drawstring sewing bag; contents: ivory bodkins, three thread bobbins, five handmade celluloid thread winders, aluminum thimble, strawberry emery, tape measure with silk print cover, shoe buttons; metal, mother-of-pearl; bottom of bag serves as a pinkeep; calling card "Mrs. Wilber F. Duffield"; $75.00.

Row two:
1. USA; Patricia silk dressmakers pins, ¼ lb., needle points; $10.00.
2. USA; silk and velvet pansy pinkeep; beautiful handwork; $48.00.
3. USA; leather fold-up for pins and needles, paper thread winders; silk lining; $50.00.

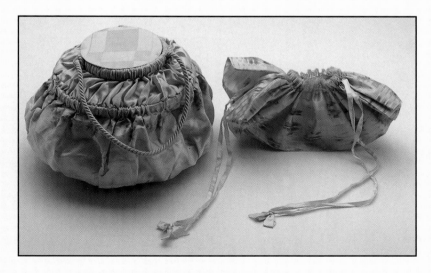

1. USA; silk print sewing bag; parts of two embroidery hoops used to shape bag, top lifts up; early twentieth century; $60.00.
2. USA; silk print drawstring sewing bag with two compartments; early twentieth century, silk has some splitting; $30.00.

145

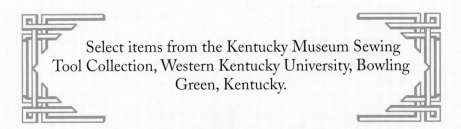

Select items from the Kentucky Museum Sewing Tool Collection, Western Kentucky University, Bowling Green, Kentucky.

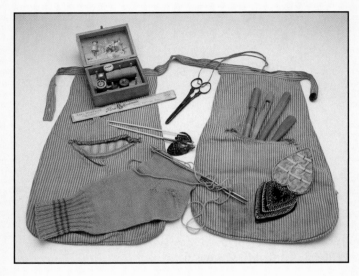

Top row:
1. Clark's ONT thread; label inside the top "is the best," boys playing games with spools of thread; Mauchline wood box; outfitted with eight spindles for thread, thimble, holder, pincushion; c. 1900; $150.00.
2. England; cast-iron sewing scissors, neck ribbon; c. 1900; $25.00.

Row two:
1. England; "Flora Macdonald Steel Knitting Pins" "Abel Morrall's Over a Century's Reputation" "Set 14"; c. 1875; NPA.
2. Knitting needle sheath; handmade for short needles;
3. Four wood sewing items; needle case, netting needle, punch, marking press; in pocket; c. 1915; $12.00 each.

Row three:
1. Hand knit wool sock in progress; pair of steel needles.
2. Heart-shaped needle book, handmade with buttonhole stitched edging; inside fitted for packets of needles; c. 1930; $18.00.

Background:
Pair of handmade pockets worn under skirts and dresses, bound pocket opening, lined with ticking; made in Kentucky.

USA; Shaw and Clark Manufacturer; "Fat Pillar" treadle machine, excellent condition; late 1860s; with treadle value of $1,000.00 – 2,000.00; without treadle, $500.00.

Top row:
1. Shaker sewing box; bronzed leather, silk lining; attached pincushion, thimble and holder, silk thread compartment, needle book; beautiful; snap closure; NPA.
2. Shaker velvet sewing bag; silk lining and drawstrings; fold-up needle book with pocket, velvet pincushion, emery with real acorn cap and ribbon; the bag is handmade, hand quilted with embroidered edges; NPA.

Row two:
1. Silk covered pincushion; decorative "pulled work," china hunting hound; c. 1920; $38.00.
2. Paper needle holder, advertisement; c. 1900; $10.00.

USA; New England type; treadle base; c. 1860 – 1870s; good condition; $500.00 – 750.00.

These items in the formal living room represent different countries and periods of history. The table is a sewing table that houses spools of thread inside under the top, look closely at the lower left-hand corner, there are small holes that the thread comes out of, the spools are all the way around allowing more than one sewer access to thread; center storage is divided into sections; Pat. 1872; $350.00.

Clockwise:
1. Two-color bamboo sewing baskets, blue silk lining; painted and glass peachblow darners; c. 1920, 1890; $300.00.
2. England; Victorian thread stand, walnut, storage drawer; six spindles with thread; decorative glass and mother-of-pearl pin-heads; c. 1875; $95.00.
3. Round sewing box, black and tan finish with metal trim; attached to top is a sewing bird, four thread spindles, two spools of thread, thimble spindle and metal thimble; NPA.
4. Asia; vegetable ivory pincushion, pierced work; c. 1860; $60.00.
5. England and USA; six pincushion shoes; three gilded with souvenir medallions; one copper finish, two nickel finish, one miniature brown finish; c. 1900; $10.00 – 60.00 each.
6. England; lady's companion, round leather with brass trim, decorative brass top; cut steel tools; c. 1850; $225.00.
7. Asia; vegetable ivory tape measure; ivory turn spindle, cloth tape; coquille palm nut; c. 1850; $60.00.
8. USA; gun-metal buttonhole scissors in leather sheath; tracing wheel; c. 1875; $50.00.
9. Steel buttonhole scissors, brass screw for enlarging; c. 1900; $35.00.
10. England; red velvet thimble holder; c. 1900; $45.00.
11. Brass trunk thimble holder; c. 1910; $50.00.
12. USA; tatting sample with mother-of-pearl winder, needle case, abalone crochet hook, punch, winder, tape measure, tatting shuttles abalone, steel, brass; c. 1880; $10.00 – 75.00 each.
13. Asia; vegetable ivory tape measure; made from a corozo palm seed; ivory turn spindle; cloth tape; c. 1860; $50.00.
14. England; lady's shoe pincushion and thimble; decorative beading shoe and sole; c. 1900; $35.00.
15. Germany; German silver base, crying child, spindle for thimble and sterling thimble; c. 1880; $200.00.

Scotland; tartan ware sewing items in a wood tartan ware box; colors of tartans are similar but designs distinguish clan identity; master bedroom display.
1. Book of Burn's poems, portrait medallion on cover; needle case, thread holder, pinkeep, tape measure, thread holder, needle book wool pages;
2. Three thread boxes; eyelets for thread release on side of first, through top on two, Burn's statue on top of three; pincushion in corner;
3. Pincushion, darner, glove stretchers, sewing kit egg, darner, long needle case; NPA.

USA; Shaker style thread box; all wood except hardware; the darker wood is the top of box, the light wood swings out to close side, black latch secures the box; spools of silk and cotton sewing thread; c. 1910; NPA.

Formal living room table display.
Top row:
1. USA; hand-painted china bowl; china painting was very popular with upper middle class women during fourth quarter of nineteenth century and early twentieth century.
2. Victorian photo box; painted portrait and garland on celluloid; c. 1880.

Row two:
1. Turned wood, two-tier thread holder; silk thread; c. 1875; $110.00.
2. Two pot-metal boot pincushions; c. 1900; $45.00 – 65.00 each.

Ceramic shoe pincushion; Victorian reproduction; $50.00.

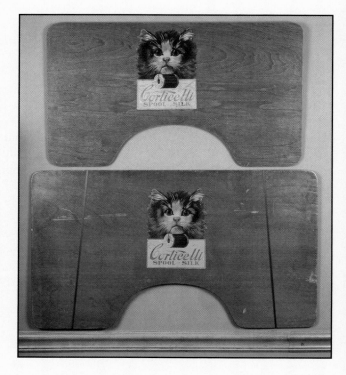

Wall display in family room; pair of red stained plywood sewing lap boards; Corticelli silk thread label, cat holding thread in mouth; $150.00 each.

These items are on display in the playroom of the collectors home along with some toy sewing machine.
1. USA; cross-stitch canvas and material displayed under the box lid.
2. USA; skirt, blouse, and fabrics; celluloid sewing doll, scissors, thimble, two pieces of fabric, embroidery hoop and wool yarn; metal latch to secure the box when closed; c. 1950; $50.00 – 75.00.

USA; Dolly Dear sewing kit with instructions on the inside of case lid; also two packets of needles, thread, and one card of mother-of-pearl buttons; first row four different fabrics and paper patterns; composition doll, blond painted hair and blue eyes; third row four different fabrics and patterns; cotton thread and aluminum thimble; four paper patterns; red and white additional dress patterns; original box and contents; Mfr. "Transogram Co. NY" stamped 1930; $100.00 – 125.00.

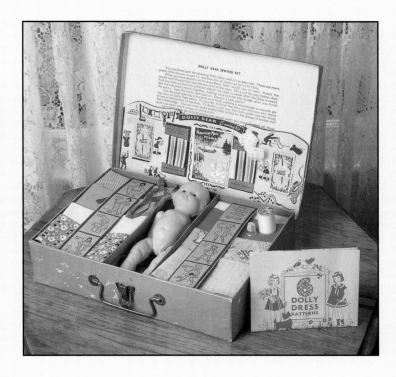

USA; a Lynn Pressman Original, design: Milton Herder; sewing bag original box; patterns, wedding dress, going away dress; "look for doll under the tray"; scissors, plastic thimble, purple ribbon, packets of pins and needles, pincushion with emery, two spools of thread, 36" tape measure, snaps; the bag is secured with a snap strap; c. 1950; $125.00 – 150.00.

The beautiful display case was handcrafted by the collector's husband; it has lighting installed; the value range of the toy machines in this case is $300.00 – 2,500.00.

Top row:
1. Germany; Pfaff, gold lettering, black finish; display card Pfaff company information in German; c. 1925.
2. Germany; Casige #204, sheet metal; four German made, wooden needle cases, c. 1930.
3. Germany; Mueller, "Mary"; small sheet metal toy; c. 1894 - 97.

Row two:
1. Germany; Casige #13; cast iron with sheet metal base; decorative gold work; doll seated at miniature treadle machine; words on arm "Lucky Baby" wind up toy.
2. Germany; Casige #3; cast iron, decorative gold work; c. 1900.
3. "Pony," cast iron, enameled and gold work; very similar to the Foley and Williams machines, two different listing as to their location Chicago and Kankakee, Illinois; small leather boot pincushion, elephant tape measure, and pincushion; c. 1900; $20.00 – 40.00.

Row three:
1. USA; American "Gem," long thin legs; decorative gold work, some letters missing; cast iron; small boy pincushion at base.

Row four:
1. Poland; Lilliput; sheet metal; original box behind machine.
2. USA; Triumph; frame made of wood with metal parts; enameled and floral designs; fastens to table with clamp; this toy machine is relatively scarce.
3. Germany; Casige #212; sheet metal, hollow arm; attractive red and gold designs; mounted on wood base; c. 1920.

This display contains a part of toy sewing machine collection. The value range of the sewing machines is $100.00 – 200.00.

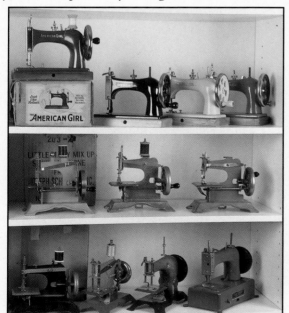

Master bedroom display shelves made by the husband of the collector; only one section is presented.

Top row:
1 – 4. American Girl sewing machines; one original box displayed; made by "National Sewing Machine Co."; c. 1930.

Row two:
1 – 3. "Little Mary," sheet metal; Joseph Scheiner Mfr. Inc., NY; c. 1930.

Row three:
1, 2. USA; Little Princess, sheet metal, flat arms;
3, 4. USA; Hoge Mfr. Co., NY; Little Princess, hollow arms.

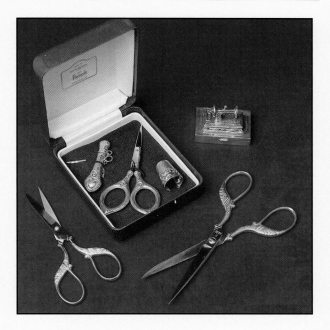

The following items are displayed in the family room.

Top row:
1. USA; this charming "Time Out" doll made for both boys and girls became popular in the 1990s; $75.00.
2. USA; "Daisy SMCO, Cleveland, O, Patented July 3, 1883, No. 2562"; cast-iron treadle frame, gold lettering of manufacturer, daisy medallions on each side; wood table top 17½" x 10"; machine cover called a bonnet or coffin, matches the table; the name is "Little Daisy"; $200.00.
3. USA; miniature pressed glass lamp on machine table; c. 1900; $75.00.
4. USA; pair of child's shoes on treadle pedal; c. 1920; $45.00.

Row two:
1. USA; child's wood sewing box; slant top on each side and handle, painted rose, footed stand; c. 1930; $35.00.
2. USA; a pair of 1930 cloth dolls, girl and boy; seated in child's spindle back straight chair; c. 1920; $60.00 pair.

USA; chatelaine, sterling; ornate clip medallion with perched crane; five chains of small shield chain links; second and fourth joined by small medallion; needle case, Webster Co. thimble holder, capped strawberry emery, pencil monogram "ATB," needle case reproduction; c. 1900; $1,000.00 – 2,000.00.

Top row:
1. England; Harrods; made by "Am D Normann" sterling silver; needle case with chain, embroidery scissors, thimble with gold lining; late 1990s; $90.00.
2. England; Harrods; sterling pin box, miniature sewing machine on top; late 1990s; $85.00.

Row two:
1. Germany; Hinckels Mfr.; embroidery and dress-makers scissors, gilded handles; c. late 1990s; $45.00.

USA; "The ladies favorite tracing wheel"; wheel is cardboard; metal chalk holder attached to wood handle; "Boston, MA. manufactured by Novelty Wheel Co, Pat. Oct. 23, 1877"; $150.00.

England; sewing bird, silver plate; one pincushion on "C" clamp; stamped designs; c. 1850; 3" x 3½"; $200.00.

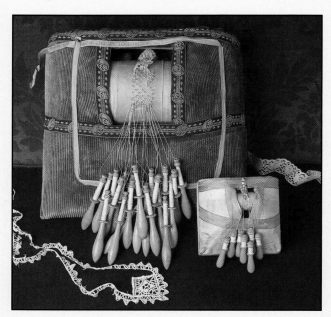

Lacemaking pillow of corduroy with braid and ribbon trim; lace design on roller, straight pins are set on pattern; $350.00.

Small lacemaking pillow used for teaching children; starched fabric with ribbon trim; $100.00 – 250.00 each.

USA, Nashville; sewing room; expandable wire mesh, steel central post and stand, female manikin for dressmaking, darners made of wood, plastic; handles that hold pins and needles, clear glass; majority were made in USA, others Germany, England; c. 1900 – 1940; $10.00 – 40.00.

This display is located in the living room of a 1724 New England home. It stands at one end of the mantel over the fireplace. The raised panels are storage. Note the Wilson-Wheeler sewing machine on the mantel, and three Somerset pottery pieces on the floor.

On top of the upper store display case there is different styles of thread holders, also called thread stands. The lettering on drawers "new six cord, spool cotton" does not identify the manufacturer. The glass doors allow for attractive displays and drawers for easy access. These two cases were used in general merchandise stores, in some areas of the US through the 1940s.

The lower case drawer lettering "100 Yards," "Spools," "Silks," "Button Hole," "Twist," "Corticelli." The two glass storage shelves house thimbles representative of at least 18 countries and range in age from 1890 to 1980. They are made of brass, aluminum, sterling silver, enamel, leather, steel, Bakelite, china, ivory, and plastic. The eight drawers have attractive and diverse displays of tools. This short list represents a lot of social history, and prices do not include display cases.

"Little Masterpieces" etched on front glass panel is a countertop inventory display case. Additional Mauchline and tartan ware; carved Black Forest; glass-eyed bear thimble holder and pincushion; beautiful German scissors and sheath; $110.00 – 400.00 each.

On the table in the foreground is an interesting collection of sewing clamps made of iron, steel, brass, silver. Note the variety of styles of the birds; beaks open to hold fabric, four do not have pincushions. There is one that has a thread bobbin attached and a free-arm pincushion, heart thumbscrew, the bird is stylized. Grouping c. 1790 – 1900; $150.00 – 750.00 each.

Two beautifully outfitted French sewing boxes, wood, inlay, and silk lining. Three leather outfitted sewing kits, top and right French, leather cases all three, two silver one gold; NPA.

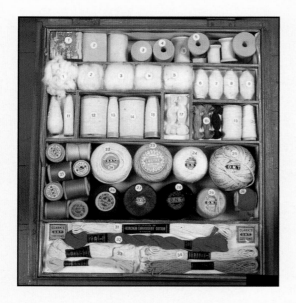

Display of Clark's ONT thread manufacturing process and product ready for sale. Top row, blocks of wood used to make spools, raw cotton processed from fiber to thread for sewing, crocheting, darning, and embroidery, bleached and dyed thread. Sewing thread put on wood spools, other threads on cardboard spools. An original display; NPA.

This countertop case, "Brainard Armstrong Thread Box," has the Simons Bros. sterling silver display thimble made for the World's Columbian Exposition of 1892 in Chicago, IL. The case contains three glass front drawers with a wide variety of Mauchline ware tools and other useful items; NPA.

"The Oakville Co. NE Plus Ultra Pins" countertop case, Mauchline ware boxes and assorted smalls. Drawers 1 – 6 have glass fronts. The large sterling Simons Bros. thimble was made to display at the World's Columbian Exposition in 18892, held in Chicago, IL; NPA.

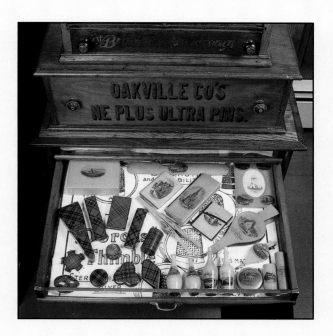

The drawer is lined with a paper advertisement for Dorcas Thimbles. On display are 16 pieces of Mauchline ware and ten pieces of tartan ware. Note the beautiful etching transfer of Scot Monument, Edinburgh, and the tartan clover-shaped pinkeep; $100.00 – 400.00.

Pictorial paper needle books of varying sizes. They were for handouts, fund raising door to door, and advertising. There are two die-cuts that are popular items, "A & P" and "Worcester Iodized Salt." Grouping c. 1880 – 1945; $10.00 – 85.00.

The following photographed trays were removed from the case in order to show additional tools that are a part of this collection.

Four bone handle crochet hooks, one button hook. Bakelite sewing kits, the top is thimble, many used for travel. Figural kits include children, tree, bird, dogs, and lion; seven different tatting shuttles, a variety of other smalls in the attractive display; $20.00 – 250.00.

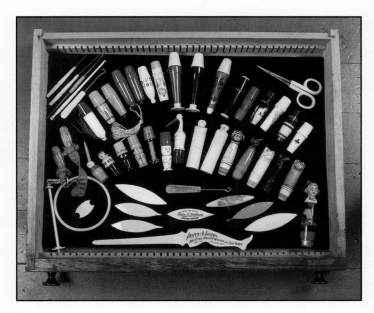

Paper pin and needle packets, "Prince Albert"; Milward needles, scene of Fountainbleu. Clark's ONT die-cut advertisement shape of a spool. Five Prudential pinkeeps, 1915 – 1930. Butterfly silk pinkeep. Needle packet with Columbian Exposition symbols and an entry ticket to the Exposition 1st of May to 30th October, 1893, mint condition; $35.00 – 75.00 each.

Grouping of eight thimble holders, six shell brass trim, one sweet grass, and one French pressed brass. Sterling thimbles and display box; cat and two owls with glass eyes thimble holders; lacemaking bobbins with a ring of seven glass beads; ivory glove stretchers, two Dorcas thimbles and box; medal, embossed medallion pinkeep; silver capped red "strawberry" thread waxer, crane and reeds on enameled pinkeep; hand-carved wooden man's shoe; variety of pincushions, fern ware thread holder, carved Black Forest, glass-eyed bear thimble holder; $40.00 – 250.00 each.

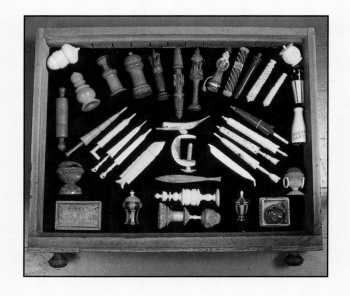

The majority of this exhibit is needle holders, they are made of ivory, vegetable ivory, wood, beaded, and made in England, Asia, France, Italy. Three vegetable ivory pincushions, two beautiful stick ware holders, ivory thimble holder and thread holder; $65.00 – 300.00 each.

Glossary

Bodkin: a blunt needle or flat tool with a long, slender eye for drawing ribbon, tape, or braid through casings or hems and lace.

Brass: copper base alloy with zinc as the alloying agent.

Bronze: one of the earliest alloys made by man, in common use by 100 BC. It was used for tools as well as decorative items. Bronze is an alloy of copper, tin, and largely magnesium.

Celluloid: developed in 1856 from land plants, cotton, straw, jute, etc., a compound of cellulose nitrate and camphor. Manufactured in 1868 and often identified with novelty items and souvenirs.

Emboss: to adorn with raised decorative pattern. Pressure is applied against a steel die roll cut or engraved with a pattern.

Emery: used as abrasive, a dark granular corundum used for polishing and grinding and fill for pincushions.

Etui: French, small kit containing tools for sewing and/or personal use.

Filigree: ornamental, open work of delicate, intricate designs.

Gold Fill: items made of a base metal overlaid with gold.

Jasperware: an unglazed vitreous fine stoneware. Mineral oxides are used to produce different colors. Wedgwood, the developer, has been in business since 1794.

Knitting: the creation of items by a series of intermeshing loops of yarn one row at a time using slender needles of varying sizes.

Lace: a patterned ornamental, open-work fabric.

Lady's Companion: a small carrying box of tools (see Necessaire).

Latten: an alloy of calamine, zinc carbonate, and copper resembling brass, hammered into thin sheets.

Lead: a bluish, white metallic element often used in combinations creating alloys.

Lusterware: earthenware decorated by applying to the glaze the metallic compounds which become iridescent metallic films when fired.

Mother-of-Pearl: a hard, pearly iridescent inner layer of a fresh/or salt water mollusk shell, used for many different personal, household, and sewing items.

Nails: a measure of fabrics and ribbons during the mid-1900s, equivalent to our 2¼" measure.

Necessaire: a carrying case for small items, such as sewing, personal, and/or writing and drawing tools. They appeared in sales catalogs in the mid-1700s.

Nickel Plate: a thin layer of nickel joined by electrolysis to an object made of other metals to improve their finish and prevent rust.

Nickel Silver: a hard, tough alloy of nickel, copper, and zinc and is sometimes called "German silver," capable of a high polish.

ONT: "our new thread," Clark Co. Best Spool Cotton.

Patents: relating to or concerned with granting of patents especially for inventions.

Repoussé: shaped or ornamented with patterns in relief made by hammering, or pressing on reverse side, used in metal work.

Solder: an alloy of lead and tin used to join metal surfaces.

Stanhope: a very small glass rod about ¼" long that one can look through and see various magnified black and white scenes. The inventor was Charles Stanhope, 3rd Earl of Stanhope (1753 – 1816). Stanhopes were decorative items in needlework tools from 1860 to 1915.

Stereograph: a picture composed of two superimposed stereoscopic images that gives a 3-D effect when viewed with a stereoscope.

Sterling: represents a standard of quality, 925 parts silver with 75 parts of copper. Abbreviations seen stamped on items are "ster.," "stg.," "stig.," "str.," or "ss."

Tin: a lustrous low melting element that is used as a protective coating in tin foil, soft solder, and alloys.

Vegetable Ivory: the corozo nut of a South American palm tree. The nut contains seeds that are the color and texture of ivory. When exposed to the light they turn a honey color. It is also called ivory nut and tagua nut. In use sine 1700s by carvers and turners. The coquilla nut that comes from a Brazilian palm is about the size of a hen's egg. Because of its hardness, it has been popular with turners of small objects since the 1500s. The shell of the coquilla was used to make small items, many of which were sewing items. The carving properties of both corozo and coquilla identify them with ivory.

Bibliography

Banister, Judith. *English Silver Hallmarks.* London: W. Foulsham & Co. Ltd., 1900.

Cummins, Genevieve E. and Nerylla D. Tauton. *Chatelaines, Utility to Glorious Extravagance.* England: Antique Collector's Club, 1994.

Encyclopedia Americana International Edition, The. Danbury, Connecticut: Grolier Incorporated, 1991, Volume 16.

Encyclopedia Britannica. Volume 8, 1995.

Fryer, Jane Eayre, *Mary Frances Sew Book.* Philadelphia, PA: The John C. Winston Company, First Edition, 1913. Reissue, Berkley, CA: Lacis, 1997.

Gullers, Barbara. *Antique Sewing Tools and Tales.* United States and Sweden: 1992.

Houart, Victor. *Sewing Accessories, an Illustrated History.* London: Souvenir Press Ltd., 1984.

Johnson, Eleanor. *Needlework Tools, a Guide to Collecting.* England: Shire Publications Ltd., 1987.

Leopold, Allison Kyle. *Cherished Objects. Living with and Collecting Victoriana.* USA: C. Potter Publishers, 1988.

McConnel, Bridget. *The Story of Antique Needlework Tools.* Atglen, PA: Schiffer Publishing Ltd, 1999.

McManus, Michael. *A Treasury of American Scrimshaw.* New York, NY: Penguin Books, USA Inc., 1997.

Muller, Wayne. *Darn It! The History and Romance of Darners.* Indiana: L & W Book Sales, 1995.

Ormsbee, Thomas H. *Field Guide to American Victorian Furniture.* New York, NY: Bonanza Books, 1953.

Pickford, Ian. *Jackson's Hallmarks, Pocket Edition.* England: Antique Collectors' Club Ltd., 1993.

Rainwater, Dorothy T. *Encyclopedia of American Silver Manufacturers.* Atglen, PA: Schiffer Publishing Ltd., 1986.

Rogers, Gay Ann. *Illustrated History of Needlework Tools.* London: Johny Murray (Publishers) Ltd., 1989.

Thomas, Glenda. *Toy and Miniature Sewing Machines.* Paducah, KY: Collector Books, 1995.

Tuaton, Nerylla. *Antique Needlework Tools and Embroideries.* Wood Bridge, Suffolk: Antique Collectors' Club Ltd., 1997.

Wallace, Carol McD. *Victorian Treasures, an Album and Historical Guide for Collectors.* New York, NY: Harry Abrams, Inc., 1993.

Warren, Geoffer. *A Stitch in Time: Victorian and Edwardian Needlecraft.* England: David and James, 1976.

Webster's Seventh New Collegiate Dictionary. Springfield, Massachusetts: G & C Merriam Company, 1965.

Whiting, Gertrude. *Tools and Toys of Stitchery.* New York, NY: Columbia University Press, 1928.

World Book Encyclopedia, The. Chicago: World Book, Inc. 1985, Volume 12.

Zalkin, Estelle. *Thimble and Sewing Implements.* Pennsylvania: Warman Publishing Co., 1988.

Quarterly Magazines and Newsletters

Halket, Connie. "Black Forest Bruins," *Thimble Collectors International,* Winter 2000.

Jary, Linda. "Emeries," *Sampler and Antique Needlework Quarterly.* Hoffman Media, Inc.

Moore, Paula. "The First Patented Thimble," *Sampler and Antique Needlework Quarterly.* Arlington, TX: Hoffman Media, Inc., pages 41 and 58 – 64, Fall 2000.